Praying & Praising Mama

21 Days of Covering Your Kids in Prayer

By Carol Lee Richardson

ISBN 978-1-7348835-0-3 (eBook)
ISBN 978-1-7348835-1-0 (Paperback)

Cover Design by Ace Book Covers
Book Formatting by Word-2-Kindle

Let's Connect!
Website: www.carolleerichardson.com
Instagram: carol.lee.richardson
Facebook Group: Praying & Praising Mamas
Email: carol.lee.writes@gmail.com

DEDICATIONS

To my Lord and Savior, Jesus: You are my one true hope! Thank You for bringing me out of darkness and into the light. You have my heart! All glory, honor, and praise are Yours.

To my husband, Michael: You have been by my side each step of our journey together. Through the hills and the valleys, holding my hand and wiping my tears. Pulling me close when there were no words for the joy or sadness we were feeling. You have loved me through it all. Thank you for believing in me and encouraging me to write what God had placed in my heart. I love you.

To my children, Shaelyn, Mackenzie & Jake: I am forever grateful that the Lord allowed me to bring you into this world and hold you in my arms and my heart. I hope you know that this praying mama has been interceding for you with fervent prayers that are full of love and hope. God's words have been spoken and His promises have been proclaimed over you. May you always remember that you are dearly loved.

To my future grandchildren: Your Mimi loves you and will be covering you in prayer faithfully!

To Mom & Dad: Thank you for introducing me to the love of our Heavenly Father as a child and helping me to pray my first prayers. Also, I am grateful that you gave me the best siblings that a girl could hope for in April, Julie & Ron! The faithful love, encouragement, and support of the Thompson Family has been such a gift in my life. I love you!

To Susan & Susan: I am so grateful that the Lord has knit our lives and hearts together over the years. The love, laughter, and friendship we have shared is woven into the fabric of my life story. Thank you for being in my corner cheering me on!

To the "special forces" prayer warriors of PPAC: What an honor and privilege it has been praying & praising with you and trusting the Lord in all things. I am so grateful for your love and friendship. Thank you for standing in the gap with me.

TABLE OF CONTENTS

How to Use This Book

Welcome! I am so glad that you are joining me as we answer God's call to prayer! Together, we can lift up our prayers & praises as we commit to this 21-day challenge to cover our kids in scripture-based prayers.

Let's get started!

<u>Who</u>: Praying & Praising Mama is for any mom (biological, adoptive, foster, stepmom), grandmother, aunt, teacher, mentor or ministry worker that has children whom they love and desire to cover in intercessory prayer. Let's do this!

<u>What</u>: We will be offering up daily prayers for our children and for ourselves. We will proclaim scriptural declarations and promises over our children's lives because God's Word is powerful, and it is alive! Also, we will focus on different aspects of God's character and offer praises, because He is worthy and praise is powerful in spiritual warfare! Finally, there will be questions to ponder - by yourself or in a group setting.

<u>Where</u>: Alone in your quiet place or in a prayer group. Or both. Because quiet time is good, but fellowship and accountability have their perks too! This can be in person or online. (Consider joining me in the Facebook Group, Praying & Praising Mamas)

<u>When</u>: Umm, now. Go! Seriously, anytime of the month is a great time to begin the challenge. Just try your best to commit for 21 days in a row! My hope is that Praying & Praising Mama will encourage you to regularly incorporate scripture-based prayers into your quiet time with the Lord.

<u>Why</u>: Because God wants us to come to Him in prayer and abide in Him! He wants us to partner with Him so He can unleash His power and make miracles happen. We praise Him because He is awesome, His grace is amazing, and He alone is worthy! Finally, we are in a battle. We want to use the authority and power given to us in Christ to defeat the schemes of the devil. We do our part and pray and praise like the Lord has asked. We leave the results to Him. Spoiler alert: God answers prayers and you will see Him do amazing things!

A few more thoughts from my head & heart:

(1) These prayers, scriptural declarations, and praise points are most powerful when you speak them out loud! Sure, you can pray them silently! Of course, God will hear your prayers whether they are silent or spoken. But there is so much power when we actually voice them out loud!

(2) It will probably feel awkward! When I first started praying God's Word over my children and proclaiming scriptural declarations out loud, it felt weird. But when I experienced the power that came with declaring these truths out loud with confidence, I was hooked!

(3) What was even more uncomfortable & awkward at first was declaring Scriptures over my children as if they were true, when in fact some had not yet come to fruition. I wondered if it was dishonest or wrong to be speaking God's truths and promises over my kids as if they were already present in their lives! However, I soon came to realize that God was more than fine

with this! He wants us to step out in faith and boldly declare His Word and His will for our children. He desires for His power to be released into their lives. We are to walk by faith and not by sight! We may not see the fruit in our children yet, but the harvest is coming! We are never wrong to pray and proclaim God's Word over our loved ones as if it were already so.

(4) I really debated about which pronouns to use in my scripture-based prayers and scriptural declarations. I decided to go with the plural pronouns so women could pray over multiple children at once. However, I do recognize that there are lots of moms who have one child by choice or would like to have more children but are struggling with infertility. And sadly, there are moms who have lost a child or several children. Please know that I recognize that families come in all sizes and I do care about moms & families who have been through the pain of infertility, miscarriage, stillbirth, infant loss, or the loss of an older child. I am so grateful you want to be a part of this prayer journey. You will simply insert singular pronouns when praying for your child. Thank you for your understanding. I am joining you in prayer!

(5) My hope is that this prayer guide will be encouraging to you and will inspire you to compose your own scripture-based prayers with your favorite Bible verses and promises of God! Praying scripture is a strategic and powerful way to pray and I hope you will find that it also strengthens your faith. But don't forget to also regularly have conversations with the Lord where you simply share your heart with Him! He delights when we spend time with Him and draw near. God rejoices when we seek Him in prayer, whether it is free-style or more structured, such as in scripture-based prayers! Just keep praying! The Lord will be faithful to answer.

Inspirational Insights

"I remember my mother's prayers and they have always followed me. They have clung to me all my life."

~ Abraham Lincoln

"Prayer is not overcoming God's reluctance. It is laying hold of His willingness."

~ Martin Luther

"Our prayers lay the track down which God's power can come. Like a mighty locomotive, His power is irresistible, but it cannot reach us without rails."

~ Watchman Nee

"God is waiting to be put to the test by His people in prayer. He delights in being put to the test on His promises. It is His highest pleasure to answer prayer, to prove the reliability of His promises."

~ Edward McKendree Bounds

"To pray without expectation is to misunderstand the whole concept of prayer and relationship with God."

~ A.W. Tozer

"Prayer is where the action is."

~ John Wesley

"The Word of God is like a lion. You don't have to defend the lion. All you have to do is let the lion loose, and the lion will defend itself."
~ Charles Spurgeon

"When you cannot rejoice in feelings, circumstances or conditions, rejoice in the Lord."
~ A.B. Simpson

"When you want to work for God, start a committee. When you want to work with God, start a prayer group."
~ Corrie Ten Boom

"Why do so many Christians pray such tiny prayers when their God is so big?"
~ Watchman Nee

"Every mighty move of the Spirit of God has had its source in the prayer chamber."
~ E.M. Bounds

"When joy and prayer are married, their first-born child is gratitude."
~ Charles Spurgeon

"Pray often, for prayer is a shield to the soul, a sacrifice to God, and a scourge for Satan."
~ John Bunyan

"God dwells in the heart where praise is."
~ A.W. Tozer

"Prayer turns ordinary mortals into men of power. It brings power. It brings fire. It brings rain. It brings life. It brings God."
~ Samuel Chadwick

INTRODUCTION

Words matter. Prayer changes things. Praise is powerful.

<u>Words matter</u>! Written or spoken, they are powerful. Think about how the words spoken to you or written about you have impacted your life... for the better or for the worse. Words have the power to create, inspire, heal, encourage, edify, and embolden. They can also hurt, damage, discourage, dishearten, and destroy.

God spoke the world into existence. Think about it! God created the heavens and the earth with His words. That is some serious creative power that exists and is made manifest by God's words! The scriptures reveal to us that "In the beginning was the Word, and the Word was with God, and the Word was God. He was with God in the beginning. Through Him all things were made; without Him nothing was made that has been made" (John 1:1-3 NIV). Jesus literally is the Word of God! That means that there is an amazing, unfathomable, life-changing power in the Holy Scriptures! The Word of God is living and active (Hebrews 4:12 ESV)! Therefore, it is so important for us to read and study God's Word and infuse it into our prayers. As we share our hearts with the Lord and speak His words and promises as we offer our prayers, there is a great outpouring of His power!

The Word of God also instructs us that death and life are in the power of the tongue (see Proverbs 18:21 ESV). While the Lord is all-powerful and none compare to Him, He wants us to know that our words are powerful too! The Lord desires for us to comprehend the gravity and the impact of our words and to choose them carefully. Truly, the words that we speak and write have consequences. Will we choose to speak life-giving words? Will we wield their power wisely and with love? Will we offer them up in passionate, powerful prayers? Will we choose to speak blessings over others or curses? Will our utterances nourish life and nurture growth? What legacies will we create with our words in the lives of our children?

God himself invites us to draw near to Him in prayer. To spend time with Him and abide. To confess our sins. To offer thanksgiving and praises. He lovingly invites us to be in relationship with Him and to share our hearts with Him. But He also invites us into prayer so that we can partner with Him. Take a moment and really soak that in! God wants us to partner with Him. In His sovereignty, He has chosen to work in us and through us as we offer up our prayers to Him. Prayer is a priority to God! He has a lot to say about it in His Word:

And pray in the Spirit on all occasions with all kind of prayers and requests. With this in mind, be alert and always keep on praying for all the Lord's people. (Ephesians 6:18 NIV)

Then you will call upon Me and come and pray to Me, and I will hear you. (Jeremiah 29:12 ESV)

Watch and pray that you may not enter into temptation. The spirit indeed is willing, but the flesh is weak. (Matthew 26:41 ESV)

Rejoice in hope, be patient in tribulation, be constant in prayer. (Romans 12:12)

Likewise, the Spirit helps us in our weakness. For we do not know what to pray for as we ought, but the Spirit himself intercedes for us with groanings too deep for words. (Romans 8:26 ESV)

Do not be anxious about anything, but in every situation, by prayer and petition, with thanksgiving, present your requests to God. (Philippians 4:6 NIV)

Devote yourselves to prayer, being watchful and thankful. (Colossians 4:2 NIV)

Therefore, confess your sins to each other and pray for each other so that you may be healed. The prayer of a righteous person is powerful and effective. (James 5:16 NIV)

* This is not an exhaustive compilation of verses on prayer. Please consider doing a study for yourself exploring the many scriptures pertaining to prayer and intercession.

Prayer changes things! As we enter into prayer with the Lord, we are changed and so are the lives of the people we pray for as His power is released and His will is accomplished! When we weave the Word of God into our prayers, we can be confident that we are praying God's will and that He will be faithful to move in lives and situations.

We can all agree that God calls us to a life of prayer and that prayer is life-changing! This is true as evidenced in the Word of God. But we also need to view it considering the role it plays in spiritual warfare - because we are in a battle. For your life. For my life. For the lives of our children and all those we love. This battle is fought in the spiritual realm. We may not be able to see it with our eyes, but it is real and so is the enemy of our souls. The Word of God tells us that "the thief comes to steal, kill, and destroy" (see John 10:10 NIV). The Lord also cautions us, "Be alert and of sober mind. Your enemy the devil prowls around like a roaring lion looking for someone to devour" (see 1 Peter 5:8 NIV). The reality is that we live in a sinful and fallen world and the enemy wants us to lose hope and turn our backs on God. He is deceitful, cunning, and full of empty promises. Make no mistake, he is hell-bent on causing death and destruction. What he desires most is for us to be separated from God for eternity. But we do not need to despair or be fearful! There is good news found in the Gospel message of Jesus Christ. We don't have to be overcome by his darkness. We can replace the lies of the enemy with the truth of God's Word. We can choose to be victors rather than victims. Through faith in Jesus, we can be redeemed, born-again, and walk in the victory and freedom already secured for us. He makes a way for us to be overcomers! Lift your hands and give praise. Hallelujah! The Lamb has overcome!

I am so grateful that we can come together and offer up intercessory prayers to the Lord on behalf of the children we love. It is simple, but powerful! We go to the Lord with faith and simply pray what He has shown us to pray in His Word and He releases His power. And as we offer our intercessory prayers to the Lord, may we also bring a heart of worship that sings His praises and brings thanksgiving.

Praise is powerful! We praise God and give Him thanks because of who He is, what He is doing in our lives (circumstances), and for what He is accomplishing in our hearts. We show Him gratitude for His protection, provisions, and blessings. God is deserving of our praise and worship. We should regularly offer up our thanksgiving because He is worthy! But praise and worship are also an important part of the spiritual warfare that we engage in as intercessors. Simply put, praise is a weapon of warfare!

We see an excellent example of this in the Book of Acts where Paul and Silas have been stripped down, beaten, and thrown in jail for sharing the Gospel. They find themselves in a dark prison cell entangled in shackles and chains. Their bodies are bound but their spirits are free! There were no complaints or protests uttered, only prayers and praise. As they lifted their voices to the Lord in the singing of hymns, the earth began to tremble. The Lord's mighty power came down and an earthquake shook the foundations of the prison. The cell doors flew open and the prisoner's chains came loose. (See Acts 16:25-26 NIV) What an amazing account of what happens when God's children praise Him in the midst of the battle!

Another example of the power of praise is found in the Old Testament account of Jehoshaphat in 2 Chronicles, "After consulting the people, Jehoshaphat appointed men to sing to the Lord and to praise Him for the splendor of His holiness as they went out at the head of the army, saying: 'Give thanks to the Lord, for His love endures forever.' As they began to sing and praise, the Lord set ambushes against the men of Ammon and Moab and Mount Seir who were invading Judah, and they were defeated" (see 2 Chronicles 20:21-22). How awesome is that? God inhabited their praises and His power manifested here on earth. The battle was won!

Be assured that the battle for the hearts and minds of our children can be won too! Mama, are you ready? It is time to pray, praise and proclaim God's mighty Word! With hope-filled hearts and steadfast faith, let's bow our heads and lift our voices together as praying & praising mamas!

Praying for the Faith of Your Children

Heavenly Father,

I come before You to intercede on behalf of my children. My prayer is that my children's hearts will be softened by Your love and willing to receive the truth of your Word. Open the eyes of my children and turn them from darkness to light, and from the power of Satan to God, so that they may receive forgiveness of sins and a place among those who are sanctified by faith in You (from Acts 26:18 NIV). May they believe that your Son, Jesus, is the promised messiah that died so that they may live. Your Word says, for by grace you have been saved through faith (from Ephesians 2:8 ESV). Thank you, Lord, for that grace that you make available to each of us. May my children fully place their trust and faith in You so that they may be saved. Out of love and a heart of gratitude, may my children live a life that is set apart and consecrated to You. May they daily proclaim that "Jesus is Lord" and profess their faith boldly and unashamedly. Let their faith always shine brightly so that they may illuminate Your truths and reflect Your love to others. May their faith be evidenced in their lives by speech that is life-giving, encouraging, edifying and shares the truth in love. Enable their faith to be demonstrated daily through acts of compassion, generosity, and kindness. Empower my children to be courageous and strong and to stand firm in enduring faith. Strengthen and sustain my children so that they may fight the good fight, finish the race and keep the faith (from 2 Timothy 4:7 ESV). Lord, you are the founder and perfecter of my children's faith (from Hebrews 12:2 ESV). I trust You will bring to completion the good work that You have begun in each of them (from Philippians 1:6 ESV).

In the mighty name of Jesus, I pray! Amen.

Scriptural Declarations to Pray Over Your Children

May my children, (speak their names), be crucified with Christ so that they no longer live, but instead Christ lives in them. The lives that they now live in the body, they live by faith in the Son of God, who loved them and gave Himself for them. (from Galatians 2:20 NIV)

May my children, (speak their names), believe in You so that out of their hearts will flow rivers of living water. (from John 7:38 ESV)

May my children, (speak their names), choose the way of faithfulness and set their hearts on Your laws. (from Psalms 119:30 NIV)

May my children, (speak their names), declare with their mouths that "Jesus is Lord" and believe in theirs heart that God raised Him from the dead so that they will be saved. (from Romans 10:9 NIV)

May the God of hope fill (speak their names) with all joy and peace as they trust in You, so that they may overflow with hope by the power of the Holy Spirit. (from Romans 15:13 NIV)

May (speak their names) walk by faith and not by sight. (from 2 Corinthians 5:7 ESV)

May (speak their names) pursue righteousness, godliness, faith, love, endurance, and gentleness. (from 1 Timothy 6:11 NIV)

Praying for This Mama

Abba Father,

Lord, I believe! Help my unbelief! I love you Adonai, but sometimes doubt and worry overshadow my faith. Grow in me an unwavering faith that does not give way to circumstances. When the storms come and my world is shaking, enable me to keep my gaze steadily fixed on You. When I am overwhelmed, frightened or heartbroken, help me to cling to You and Your promises. Remind me that You will never leave or forsake me, and I do not have to figure out how to be a mom all by myself. You are patient with me and extend so much grace! Teach me Your ways, Lord and show me how to walk in them. Cultivate in me a heart that is humble and quick to repent and act on Your guidance. Lord, You are a lamp unto my feet! Strengthen and sustain me as I follow You. May I be steadfast in my faith and set apart for You. Give me the courage to stand firm on Your truths and precepts and to be a godly witness to my children. Teach me how to trust in You for all things and to fully entrust my children into Your tender loving care.

In the precious name of Jesus, I pray. Amen.

Praise Points: Praising God for His Faithfulness

Adonai, you are worthy of our praise! I love You and worship You because...

- Your steadfast love extends to the heavens, Your faithfulness to the clouds. (from Psalm 36:5 ESV)
- You are a faithful God who keeps covenant and steadfast love with those who love You and keep Your commandments. (from Deuteronomy 7:9 ESV)
- Your steadfast love never ceases! Your mercies never come to an end; they are new every morning. (from Lamentations 3:23 ESV)

What Do You Think? Questions for Reflection or Group Discussion

1. In what ways can you encourage your kids in their faith?

2. What role do you think prayer will play in building up the faith of your children? Do you ever pray out loud when proclaiming God's Word over their lives?

3. How does praying God's Word over your children change things in their hearts and lives?

4. Do your prayers for your children impact your own faith in any way? If yes, how so?

5. What doubts and fears have caused you to struggle in your faith?

6. What strategies do you use to combat your doubts and fears?

7. Do you have difficulty releasing your children to God? If yes, why do you think that is?

Praying for Your Children to Hope in the Lord

Adonai,

You are my living hope! My prayer and the cry of my heart are for my children to put all their hope in You. There are so many things in the world that can lead us away from You - temptations and fruitless endeavors that can never provide fulfillment, healing or redemption. You are our one true hope! May my children embrace that hope in You wholeheartedly and never let it be replaced by the empty promises of the world. May they praise You continually because in Your great mercy, You have given them a new birth into a living hope through the resurrection of Jesus Christ from the dead (from 1 Peter 1:3 NIV). Lord, You are the God of hope! Fill my children to overflowing with joy and peace as they trust in You (from Romans 15:13 NIV)! May the Holy Spirit enable them to hope in You even when their circumstances are difficult. Let them wait for You Lord to act in your timing. And as they wait, strengthen them to hold on unswervingly to the hope they profess, because You are faithful, and Your promises are true (from Hebrews 10:23 NIV). When the darkness of the world presses in on my children, may they run to You, their refuge and shield, and put their hope in Your Word (from Psalm 119:114 NIV). Lord, You have proclaimed that those who hope in You will renew their strength and they will soar on wings like eagles. They will run and not be weary, they will walk and not faint (from Isaiah 40:31 NIV). Strengthen my

9

children as they place their hope in You so they may endure in faith and have confidence in You and Your promises. May they look to You expectantly as Your plans for their lives unfold, for You have declared that these plans are plans to prosper them and not to harm them. You have plans to give them a hope and a future (from Jeremiah 29:11 NIV). Guide my children in Your truth and teach them, for You are their God and Savior (from Psalm 25:5 NIV), their one true hope. May Your unfailing love be with my children, Lord, as they renew their hope daily and place their trust in You.

In the name of Jesus, I pray. Amen!

Scriptural Declarations to Pray Over Your Children

(Names of your children) wait for the Lord, their whole beings wait, and in His Word they put their hope. (from Psalm 130:5 NIV)

May Your unfailing love be with (names of your children), Lord, even as they put their hope in You. (from Psalm 33:22 NIV)

Praise be to the God and Father of our Lord Jesus Christ! In His great mercy He has given (names of your children) new birth into a living hope through the resurrection of Jesus Christ from the dead. (from 1 Peter 1:3 NIV)

The Lord is the portion of (names of your children), therefore they will hope in Him. (from Lamentations 3:24 ESV)

Guide my children, (speak their names), in your truth and teach them, for You are God their Savior, and their hope is in You all day long. (from Psalm 25:5 NIV)

And hope does not put us to shame, because God's love has been poured into the hearts of my children, (speak their names), through the Holy Spirit who has been given to them. (from Romans 5:5 ESV)

I pray that the eyes and hearts of (names of your children) may be enlightened in order that they may know the hope to which He has called them, the riches of his glorious inheritance in His holy people. (from Ephesians 1:18 NIV)

Praying for This Mama

Adonai,

Create in me a steadfast faith so that I do not place my hope in worldly things or in my own strength, but instead put my hope in You. There are so many times that I doubt my ability to parent my children and I become fearful and unsure. Other times, I am heartbroken and weary as I watch my children struggle and in pain as they navigate through this world. When the darkness looms and circumstances seem overwhelming, enable me to hold onto Your promises and be reminded that You are my living hope. May my children witness me placing my hope daily in Your unfailing love. Because of You, the God of hope, I can be filled with Your joy and peace and rejoice in hope during both the good times and hard times.

In the name of Jesus, I pray, Amen.

Praise Points: Praising God for Hope

Lord, I am rejoicing in hope and filled with gratitude because...

- You bring to completion the good work that You have begun in me. (from Philippians 1:6 ESV)
- You fill me with joy and peace as I trust in You so that I may overflow with hope by the power of the Holy Spirit. (from Romans 15:13 NIV)

- When I place my hope in You, my strength is renewed. (from Isaiah 40:31 NIV)

- You have given me a new birth into a living hope through the resurrection of Jesus Christ from the dead. (from 1 Peter 1:3 NIV)

- You are my hiding place and my shield. I can place my hope in Your Word. (from Psalm 119:114 ESV)

What Do You Think? Questions for Reflection or Group Discussion

1. Have you ever felt hopeless? Which situations or circumstances have caused you to lose hope?

2. What happens when we lose hope?

3. How do praying and reading the Bible strengthen our hope in God and His promises?

4. What are the dangers of putting our hope in something other than God?

5. Why is God described as the God of hope?

6. What are some of your favorite scripture verses about hope? What about them resonates with you?

Praying for Your Children to Love the Lord Wholeheartedly

Yahweh,

I come to You humbly and lift my children up to You in prayer. The desire of this mama's heart is that my children will completely and wholeheartedly surrender their lives to You and that they would be filled with a deep, abiding love for You that fills their hearts and permeates their spirits. May this indescribable, radical love also captivate their minds and thoughts. Let this love and faithfulness never leave them and be written on the tablets of their hearts (from Proverbs 3:3 NIV). Enable this love to consume them entirely and endure all things as they trust in You completely. May this love never grow cold or be replaced by a love of the world. Empower my children to walk in Your ways, and to love and serve You with all their heart and soul (from Deuteronomy 10:12 ESV). Because of the great love that You have given to my children, may they be willing to become vessels for Your love and grace to be poured out in the lives of others. May their love for You be enduring and endeavor to accomplish Your will and bring You glory and honor.

In the precious name of Jesus, I pray, Amen.

Scriptural Declarations to Pray Over Your Children

May my children, (speak their names), love the Lord God with all their hearts and with all their souls and with all of their minds and with all of their strength. (from Mark 12:30 ESV)

May each of my children, (speak their names), fear the Lord God, walk in all His ways, and serve the Lord God with all their heart and with all their soul. (from Deuteronomy 10:12 ESV)

May my children, (speak their names), trust in the Lord and do good, dwell in the land, and befriend faithfulness. I pray that they will delight themselves in the Lord, and He will give my children the desires of their hearts. May my children commit their ways to the Lord; trust in Him, and He will act. (from Psalm 37:3-5 ESV)

Praying for This Mama

Lord,

You know my mama's heart and how very much I love my children. I know these children are a precious gift from You and that You have entrusted me with a high and noble calling to nurture, care for and train these children in Your ways. Help me Lord not to make an idol out of my children. Show me how to put You first always and to have You as the foundation of my life so that I can be the godly mother that You have called me to be. Lord, fill me to overflowing with an unwavering love and devotion to You that does not take a backseat to anyone or anything. Show me how to love You with all my heart, soul, mind, and strength! Help me to daily walk with You and to be obedient. Empower me to serve You wholeheartedly out of love and gratitude. Let the words of my mouth adore You and my deeds bring you glory and honor. As I abide in you, I know I will grow into the godly mom You have purposed for me to be.

In the mighty name of Jesus, I pray. Amen.

Praise Points: Praising God for His Love

Lord, my heart is filled with gratitude and thanksgiving because...

- Neither height nor depth, nor anything else in all creation, will be able to separate us from the love of God that is Christ Jesus our Lord. (from Romans 8:39 NIV)

- You are merciful and gracious, slow to anger and abounding in steadfast love and faithfulness. (from Psalm 86:15 ESV)

- You rejoice over me with gladness, quiet me with Your love and exult over me with loud singing. (from Zephaniah 3:17 ESV)

- You love us with an everlasting love, therefore You have continued Your faithfulness to us. (from Jeremiah 31:3 ESV)

- You pour Your love into our hearts through the Holy Spirit. (from Romans 5:5 ESV)

- Your steadfast love endures forever. (from Psalm 136:26 ESV)

- You so loved the world that You gave Your one and only Son, that whoever believes in Him shall not perish but have eternal life. (from John 3:16 NIV)

- For as high as the heavens are above the earth, so great is Your steadfast love towards those who fear You. (from Psalm 103:11 ESV)

What Do You Think? Questions for Reflection or Group Discussion

1. What do you think it means to love God with our whole heart, mind, soul, and strength? What does that look like in our daily lives?

2. Do you ever doubt God's love for you? Do you have trouble receiving it? If so, why?

3. What do we know to be true about God's love from the Bible?

4. What are some obstacles in your life that keep you from loving God wholeheartedly?

5. What are ways that you can teach your children about God's love for them?

6. How can we demonstrate God's love for people in our community?

7. What role do you think prayer can play in increasing our love for the Lord?

Praying for Your Children to Love the Word of God

Adonai,

Establish in the hearts of my children a deep and abiding love for Your Word! Reveal Yourself to them through Your Word so that they may know that all scripture is God-breathed. May they delight in reading Your promises and gain wisdom as they hide Your Word in their hearts. Show them the use of Your scriptures for teaching, rebuking, correcting and training in righteousness so that they may become servants of God equipped for every good work (from 2 Timothy 3:16-17 NIV). May they recognize the importance of using the Bible as their compass as they navigate through life. Let Your Word daily be a lamp for my children and a light on the path that they travel (from Psalm 119:105 NIV). Guide them with Your Word, Lord, for every work of God is flawless. Strengthen and sustain my children as they wait on You, Lord. May my children put their hope in Your Word (from Psalm 130:5 ESV). May they be continually reminded that the Word became flesh and made His dwelling among us and that Your Son is full of grace and truth (from John 1:14 NIV). May their love for the Word of God and their Savior grow daily! Help my children to hide Your Word in their hearts so that they may not sin against You (from Psalm 119:11 NIV).

Lord, I pray that the message of Jesus Christ will dwell richly among my children (from Colossians 3:16 NIV) and forever be on their tongues, in their hearts, and apparent in their lives.

In the mighty name of Jesus, I pray. Amen!

Scriptural Declarations to Pray Over Your Children

For the Word of God is alive and active, sharper than any double-edged sword. May it penetrate my children, (speak their names), dividing soul and spirit, joints and marrow. May it judge the thoughts and attitudes of their hearts. (from Hebrews 4:12 NIV)

May my children, (names of your children), not merely listen to the Word. May they do what it says. (from James 1:22 NIV)

Enable (names of your children) to wait on You Lord with their whole being. And in Your Word may they place their hope. (from Psalm 130:5 NIV)

May (names of your children) recognize that every word of God proves true. Thank You for being their shield as they take refuge in You! (from Proverbs 30:5 ESV)

May the message of Jesus Christ dwell richly in the hearts and lives of my children, (names of your children). Let Your wisdom teach and guide them. Fill their hearts with songs of praise and gratitude. (from Colossians 3:16 NIV)

While the grass withers and the flowers fall, the Word of God endures forever. Establish this truth in the hearts and minds of (names of your children) so that they will always trust in Your truths and promises. (from Isaiah 40:8 NIV)

Praying for This Mama

Lord,

Create in me a deep love and reverence for Your Word. May I hunger for the truth and wisdom found in the Bread of Life. Though I am often tired and overwhelmed by the demands of caring for my family and home, help me to set apart time daily to meet with You and to read Your Holy Scriptures. My hope is that my children will see me spending time with You and abiding in Your word. Sometimes my thoughts are scattered! Enable me to commit Your precepts and promises to memory and to hide them in my heart. Please Lord, help me not to get discouraged, or worse, deceived by the lies of the enemy. Empower me to hold my thoughts captive and to dwell on what You say is true. My hope is that I will daily hold onto Your promises and live out what You have taught me as a witness to my children. Thank you, Lord, for the precious gift of Your Word!

In the name of Jesus, I pray. Amen.

Praise Points: Praising the Lord for the Word of God

Abba, I praise and worship You because:

- Your Word does not return to You empty but accomplishes what You purpose. (from Isaiah 55:11 ESV)
- The words You have spoken to us are spirit and life. (from John 6:63 ESV)
- Faith comes from hearing, and hearing through the Word of Christ. (from Romans 10:17 ESV)
- Every word of God proves true. (from Proverbs 30:5 ESV)
- The word of our God will stand. (from Isaiah 40:8 ESV)

- All Scripture is breathed out by God and profitable for teaching, for reproof, for correction, and for training in righteousness, that the man of God may be competent, equipped for every good work. (from 2 Timothy 3:16-17 ESV)

What Do You Think? Questions for Reflection or Group Discussion

1. The Bible tells us that all scriptures are God-breathed. What does that mean?

2. How do we know that the Bible is true?

3. God describes the Word of God as living and active. How is it living and active in your life?

4. How can you incorporate Bible reading into your daily life?

5. How can you use the Holy Scriptures in the training of your kids? How can it help you in your role as a parent?

6. How does praying scriptures over your children change things in your life and in theirs?

7. Why is it important to memorize scripture?

Praying the Joy of the Lord for Your Children

Heavenly Father,

You are the Unchanging One! You are steadfast and my children and I can count on You and the promises in Your Word. The desire of my heart is that my children will abide in You daily so that they may be joy-filled even on the most difficult days. No matter the circumstances in their lives, may You, the God of hope, fill my children with all joy and peace as they trust in You, so that they may overflow with hope by the power of the Holy Spirit (from Romans 15:13 NIV). Let the hearts and minds of my children dwell on the words You have spoken, so that Your joy may be in them, and their joy may be full (from John 15:11 ESV). I intercede on behalf of my children so that gladness and joy will overtake them, and their sorrow and sighing will flee away. May they delight in You and abide in Your presence continually! Crown their heads with everlasting joy, Lord (from Isaiah 35:10 NIV). Daily remind my children that when they are anxious, Your consolation brings joy to the soul (from Psalm 94:19 NIV). When they are troubled, may they fix their eyes on Jesus, the pioneer and perfecter of their faith and remember that weeping may stay for the night, but rejoicing comes in the morning (from Hebrews 12:2 NIV and Psalm 30:5 NIV). Truly, your light will guide them through the darkest of times and bring comfort. May my children seek to take refuge in You and rejoice. Let them ever sing for joy and spread Your protection over them. Impart to each of them a love for You and Your name so that they may exult You (from Psalm 5:11 ESV). Make known to them that You are the path of life and that in Your presence there is fullness of joy (from Psalm 16:11 ESV). May the desire of their hearts be to daily dwell in Your presence and be glad in the Lord, shouting for joy with an upright heart that is filled with gratitude (from Psalm 32:11 ESV). May my children declare boldly that the Lord is their strength and shield as they entrust their hearts fully to You. Place a song on their lips as they leap for joy and give thanks to You (from Psalm 28:7 NIV). Finally, teach each of my children to rejoice in hope, be patient in tribulation, and to continually come to You in prayer (from Romans 12:12 ESV).

In the precious name of Jesus, I pray. Amen!

Scriptural Declarations to Pray Over Your Children

When anxiety is great within (names of children), Your consolation brings joy to their souls. (from Psalm 94:19 NIV)

Therefore, since (names of your children) are being justified by faith, they have peace with God through our Lord Jesus Christ. Through Him they have obtained access by faith into this grace in which they stand, and they rejoice in hope of the glory of God. Not only that, but my children rejoice in their sufferings, knowing that suffering produces endurance, and endurance produces character, and character produces hope, and hope does not put them to shame, because God's love has been poured into their hearts through the Holy Spirit that has been given to them. (from Romans 5:1-5 ESV)

Though (names of your children) have not seen Him, they love Him. Though they do not now see Him, they believe in Him and rejoice with joy that is inexpressible and filled with glory, obtaining the outcome of their faith, the salvation of their souls. (from 1 Peter 1:8-9 ESV)

Praying for This Mama

Adonai,

You have given me so much to be grateful for and so many reasons to rejoice! It is easy for me to give thanks and be joyful when things in my life are going smoothly and my children are happy, healthy, and thriving. It is during the seasons of suffering and sorrow that my soul can become downcast and despair in my circumstances. Show me how to abide in You during times of heartache and hardship. Teach me to trust You when my world seems to be crumbling. Help me to meditate on Your Word so that Your joy may be in me and Your joy may be full.

In the mighty name of Jesus, I pray. Amen.

Praise Points: Praising God for Joy

Lord, I come to You with thanksgiving because...

- You make known to me the path of life; in Your presence there is fullness of joy; at Your right hand are pleasures forevermore. (from Psalm 16:11 ESV)

- Weeping may tarry for the night, but joy comes with the morning. (from Psalm 30:5 ESV)

- You have turned for me my mourning into dancing; You have loosed my sackcloth and clothed me with gladness. (from Psalm 30:11 ESV)

- My spirit rejoices in You my God and Savior. (from Luke 1:47 ESV)

- When the cares of my heart are many, Your consolations cheer my soul. (from Psalm 94:19 ESV)

- You have clothed me with the garments of salvation and covered me with the robe of righteousness, I will greatly rejoice in the Lord and my soul shall exult in my God. (from Isaiah 61:10 ESV)

What Do You Think? Questions for Reflection or Group Discussion

1. How does one obtain the joy of the Lord?
2. What does it mean to experience the joy of the Lord?
3. Is it possible to experience joy even during trials and tribulation?
4. What do our lives look like when we are lacking the joy of the Lord?
5. What are some obstacles in your life that prevent you from experiencing the joy of the Lord?

Praying Repentance for Your Children

Heavenly Father,

I rejoice that we serve a loving and patient God who always keeps His promises! Lord, your Word says that You are patient with us, not wanting anyone to perish. Your desire is for each of us to come to repentance (from 2 Peter 3:9 NIV). Merciful Father, I pray for my children that do not yet know You, that You would give them a new heart and put a new spirit in them. Remove from them their hearts of stone and replace them with hearts of flesh (from Ezekiel 36:26 NIV). Penetrate the hearts of my children with a deep conviction of sin and a need to repent so that they may be forgiven. Deliver my precious ones from a love of the world and establish in them a love for the things of God. May my children draw near to You, and You will draw near to them (from James 4:8 ESV). As my children confess their sins, You are faithful and just to forgive them and purify them from their unrighteousness (from 1 John 1:9 NIV). Help my children to humble themselves daily and examine their hearts before You, so that You may reveal anything in their lives that is displeasing to You. Empower them with Your Holy Spirit to produce fruit in keeping with repentance (from Matthew 3:8 NIV) so that their words and deeds may bring You honor and glory. May my children's hearts always be filled with gratitude for the grace and forgiveness of sins that was bought with Your son's precious blood.

In the name of Jesus, I pray. Amen!

Scriptural Declarations to Pray Over Your Children

May (speak names of children) humble themselves and pray and seek Your face and turn from their sinful ways, then You will hear them from heaven, and You will forgive their sins. (from 2 Chronicles 7:14 ESV)

As (speak names of children) confess their sins; You are faithful and just and will forgive their sins and purify them from their unrighteousness. (from 1 John 1:9 NIV)

My children, (speak names of children), will confess and renounce their sins and they will find Your mercy. (from Proverbs 28:13 NIV)

May my children, (speak names of children), repent and be baptized in the name of Jesus Christ for the forgiveness of their sins and they will receive the gift of the Holy Spirit. (from Acts 2:38 ESV)

Lord, give (speak the names of your children who do not yet know the Lord) new hearts and put in them a new spirit. Remove from them their hearts of stone and give them hearts of flesh. (from Ezekiel 36:26 NIV)

Praying for This Mama

Father God,

While my focus is often on raising and training my children, help me daily to examine my own heart. Reveal to me Lord the areas that are displeasing to You and are in opposition to You and Your Word. Uproot my stubbornness, pride, and fear and expose and destroy any strongholds that keep me from growing in my faith. Help me to be sensitive to Your Holy Spirit as You show me the areas of my life that need to be pruned. Empower me to daily take the time to draw near and abide in You, so that You may abide in me. Cultivate in me a tender heart that is responsive to your correction and is teachable, so that I may be conformed into Your image. As I parent my children, help me to admit to my sins and mistakes and to demonstrate for them what it is like to be humble and repentant before You, Lord. Let me treasure the gifts of Your forgiveness and grace that I have received through faith and never take them for granted. May I always remember that your Son willingly shed His blood for the forgiveness of my sins and laid down His life so that I would have life everlasting.

In the mighty name of Jesus, I pray, Amen.

Praise Points: Praising God for the Gift of Repentance

Heavenly Father, my heart is filled with gratitude and thanksgiving because...

- As we confess our sins, You are faithful and just and will forgive our sins and purify us from unrighteousness. (from 1 John 1:9 NIV)

- You produce fruit in us when we repent. (from Matthew 3:8 NIV)

- You are gracious and merciful! If we return to You, You will not turn Your face away from us! (from 2 Chronicles 30:9 ESV)

- You are patient with us! You do not want anyone to perish. Rather, You want everyone to come to repentance. (from 2 Peter 3:9 NIV)

- When we return to You, the Lord Almighty, You return to us! (from Zechariah 1:3 NIV)

- If we humble ourselves, pray and seek Your face, and turn away from our wicked ways, You will hear from heaven and forgive our sins. (from 2 Chronicles 7:14 NIV)

- When we repent in the name of Jesus Christ for the forgiveness of our sins, we receive the gift of the Holy Spirit. (from Acts 2:38 ESV)

What Do You Think? Questions for Reflection or Group Discussion

1. What does it mean to repent?

2. How is repentance different from being sorry?

3. How can you teach your children the meaning of repentance?

4. What are some examples that the Bible gives regarding repentance?

5. What do we receive when we repent in the name of Jesus?

6. How would our nation look differently if it was to repent corporately?

7. What happens when we refuse to repent as an individual?

Praying for Your Children to be Set Apart

Heavenly Father,

May my children be consecrated and set apart for You! In Your mercy, You have called them out of darkness and into Your wonderful light (from 1 Peter 2:9 NIV). Because of You, they are children of the light and children of the day. Let my children put on faith and love as a breastplate, and the hope of salvation as a helmet (from 1 Thessalonians 5:8 NIV). Call and empower them to live a life that is holy before You. Daily conform them into Your image so they will not be influenced by the ways of the world. Anoint and equip them to do Your work as You reveal Your unique calling on their lives. Teach them that Your work must not be accomplished by might nor by power (from Zechariah 4:6 NIV), but by the Holy Spirit. As they abide in faith and seek to do Your will, may the fruit of the spirit be cultivated in their lives: love, joy, peace, patience, kindness, goodness, faithfulness, gentleness, and self-control (from Galatians 5:22-23 ESV). May my children be cleansed by You Lord so they may become vessels for honorable uses, set apart as holy, useful to the master of the house, and ready for every good work (from 2 Timothy 2:21 ESV).

In the holy and precious name of Jesus, I pray. Amen.

Scriptural Declarations to Pray Over Your Children

(Speak names of children), You are all children of the light and children of the day. You do not belong to the night or to the darkness. So then, do not be like others, who are asleep, but awake and sober. Since you belong to the day, be sober, putting on faith as a breastplate, and the hope of salvation as a helmet. For God did not appoint you to suffer wrath but to receive salvation through our Lord Jesus Christ. (from 1 Thessalonians 5: 5-6, 8-9 NIV)

But I say, (speak names of children), walk by the Spirit, and you will not gratify the desires of the flesh. (from Galatians 5:16 ESV)

(Speak names of children), will present their bodies as living sacrifices, holy and acceptable to God, which is their spiritual worship. They will not be conformed to this world but will be transformed by the renewal of their minds, that by testing they may discern what is the will of God, what is good and acceptable and perfect. (from Romans 12:1-2 ESV)

Praying for This Mama

Heavenly Father,

Holy, holy, holy! You are righteous and worthy of my devotion and praise. Teach me how to live a life that is consecrated and set apart for You! Fill me to overflowing with Your Holy Spirit so that I may walk by faith and point my children and others to You. May I live as a child of the light, for I have been delivered from the darkness of sin! Hallelujah! Transform me daily Lord, so that I become more and more like You. Let my children see evidence of the fruit of the Spirit in my life and be blessed and enriched as Your love and goodness flows through me. Empower me to give of myself sacrificially and to endeavor to do Your will daily. Remind me that it is only as I abide in You that I can be conformed into Your image and live a holy and set apart life.

In the powerful name of Jesus, I pray. Amen.

Praise Points: Praising God Because He is Holy and Righteous

Adonai, You are worthy of our praise! I love and worship You because...

- There is no one like You, majestic in holiness, awesome in glorious deeds, doing wonders. (from Exodus 15:11 ESV)

- You are the Lord my God and You are holy. (from Leviticus 11:44 NIV)

- You forgive my iniquity, heal my diseases, redeem my life from the pit and crown me with steadfast love and mercy. (from Psalm 103:3-4 ESV)

- You saved me and called me to a holy calling, not because of my works, but because of Your own purpose and grace. (from 2 Timothy 1:9 ESV)

- You have delivered me from the domain of darkness and transferred me to the kingdom of Your beloved Son, in whom I have redemption, the forgiveness of sin. (from Colossians 1: 13-14 ESV)

What Do You Think? Questions for Reflection or Group Discussion

1. What does it mean to be consecrated to God?
2. What does it mean to be children of light?
3. What does it look like to live a set apart life?
4. What is the fruit of the Spirit?
5. How does prayer play a role in helping our children to avoid conforming to the ways of the world?
6. How can we be living sacrifices unto the Lord?
7. What does it mean to be transformed by the renewing of our mind?

Praying for Your Children to have a Fear of the Lord

Heavenly Father,

Lord hear my prayer! My desire is for my children to always come before You with reverence and awe! May they not fear the world, man, or the enemy of their souls. Let their only fear be a holy fear of You, the Most High God. How blessed is everyone who fears the Lord. May my children walk in Your ways (from Psalm 128:1 ESV). How abundant are the good things that You have stored up for those that fear You, that You bestow in the sight of all, on those who take refuge in You (from Psalm 31:19). Thank You for Your goodness God and that You are a refuge for my children when they possess a fear of the Lord. I am grateful that Your precepts are constant, true, and trustworthy. I praise You because You love my children with an everlasting love and desire Your will to be accomplished in their lives. May it be so! May they worship You with a deep reverence and a holy fear. Behold, the eye of the Lord is on our children who fear Him, on those who hope in His steadfast love, to deliver their soul from death and to keep them alive in famine (from Psalm 33:18-19 ESV). You tell us in Your word that the fear of the Lord is a fountain of life, that one may avoid the snares of death (from Proverbs 14:27 ESV). May my children recognize that

You are the giver of life and their sustainer. Only You can deliver them from death! Lord, You are our help and our shield as we fear You and trust in You (from Psalm 115:11 NIV). May my children not endeavor to fight their spiritual battles in their own strength but instead put on the armor of God and allow You to be their covering. Your Word instructs us that the Son of Righteousness will rise with healing in its wings for those who fear His name (from Malachi 4:2 ESV). He will bless those who fear the Lord – both the small and the great (from Psalm 115:13 ESV). Father, may my children fear You and be blessed!

In the mighty name of Jesus, I pray. Amen!

Scriptural Declarations to Pray Over Your Children

The angel of the Lord encamps around my children, (speak their names), who fear Him, and He delivers them. (from Psalm 34:7 ESV)

He will fulfill the desire of my children, (speak their names), who fear Him. He will hear their cries and will save them. (from Psalm 145:19 NIV)

And He will be the stability of their times, a wealth of salvation, wisdom, and knowledge; the fear of the Lord is the treasure of my children, (speak their names). (from Isaiah 33:6 ESV)

For as high as the heavens are above the earth, so great is His steadfast love towards my children, (speak their names), who fear him. (from Psalm 103:11 ESV)

May my children, (speak their names), fear the Lord and trust in Him. He is their help and their shield. (from Psalm 115:11 ESV)

Praying for This Mama

Father God,

Let my spirit continually be in awe of You, the Most High God. May I have a holy fear and respect for You that is woven into the fabric of my faith. I pray that my words and actions would always bring You honor and glory. Enable me to live this reverence out in my daily life and routine so that I may model this for my children. May they witness me humbly coming before Your throne in prayer with an obedient and submissive spirit. Create in me a heart of worship that is overflowing with praise and thanksgiving for You, my Creator, Savior, Lord and King. You are my refuge, my stability, and my salvation. My hope is in You, for You are mighty to save! May Your blessings be upon me as I love, teach, discipline, and guide my children.

In the precious name of Jesus, I pray. Amen.

Praise Points: Praising God for a Holy Reverence

Abba Father, I praise and worship You because...

- The fear of the Lord is the beginning of knowledge. (from Proverbs 1:7 NIV)
- The fear of the Lord leads to life and whoever has it is satisfied; they will not be visited by harm. (from Proverbs 19:23 ESV)
- The friendship of the Lord is for those who fear Him, and He makes known to them His covenant. (from Psalm 25:14 ESV)
- Your mercy is for those who fear You. (Luke 1:50 ESV)
- Blessed is the person who fears the Lord, who greatly delights in His commandments. (from Psalm 112:1 ESV)
- You are the stability of our times, abundance of salvation, wisdom, and knowledge; the fear of the Lord is Zion's treasure. (from Isaiah 33:6 ESV)

What Do You Think? Questions for Reflection or Group Discussion

1. What does it mean to have a fear of the Lord?

2. What blessings does God have for those that fear the Lord?

3. What are the dangers of not fearing God?

4. How does having a fear of God help in our relationship with Him?

5. How can we teach our kids about the fear of the Lord?

6. How does studying scripture and praying it strengthen our fear of the Lord?

7. What type of fears does God warn us against?

Praying for Your Children to have Wisdom

Adonai,

I beseech You to endow my children with a spirit of wisdom and I pray that the breath of the Almighty would give them understanding (from Job 32:8 NIV). Establish in their hearts a love of Your sacred writings which can provide wisdom that leads to salvation through faith in Christ Jesus (from 2 Timothy 3:15 ESV). May our children have a fear of the Lord as this is the beginning of knowledge (from Proverbs 1:7 ESV). May each of my children have a teachable spirit and desire to be conformed into Your likeness. Create in them a willingness to listen to godly advice and to accept discipline so that they may be counted among the wise (from Proverbs 19:20 NIV). May they hunger and thirst for the truths found in Your Holy Scriptures. Let the Word of Christ dwell richly in the hearts of my children so they can teach and admonish one another in all wisdom, with thankfulness in their hearts to God (from Colossians 3:16 ESV). Father of glory, I implore You to grant the spirit of wisdom and revelation in the knowledge of Jesus Christ to my children, let the eyes of their hearts be enlightened, so that they may know the hope to which You have called them (from Ephesians 1:17-18 ESV). Enable my children to walk in humility as they patiently seek You and Your counsel. Help them to guard against pride and foolishness and to be slow to anger. Help them to recognize that the ways of wisdom are pleasantness and all her paths are peace (from Proverbs 3:17 ESV). May they encounter and abide in this peace daily. Your Holy Word reveals that the wisdom that comes from heaven is first of all pure; then peace-loving, considerate, submissive, full of mercy and good fruit, impartial and sincere (James 3:17 NIV). May the hearts of my children desire to embrace Your wisdom so that they may abound in these godly attributes. Compel my children to hear Your words and put them into practice like a wise man that builds his house on the rock (from Matthew 7:24 NIV). Teach my children to number their days so that they may gain a heart of wisdom (from Psalm 90:12 NIV).

In the powerful name of Jesus, I pray. Amen.

Scriptural Declarations to Pray Over Your Children

May my children, (speak their names), be encouraged in heart and united in love, so that they may have the full riches of complete understanding in order that they may know the mystery of God, namely Christ, in whom are hidden all the treasures of wisdom and knowledge. (from Colossians 2:2-3 NIV)

If my children, (speak their names), lack wisdom, they should ask God, who gives generously to all without finding fault, and it will be given to them. (from James 1:5 NIV)

Teach my children, (speak their names), to number their days, so that they may gain a heart of wisdom. (from Psalm 90:12 NIV)

My children, (speak their names), will know the truth, and the truth will set them free. (from John 8:32 ESV)

May my children, (speak their names), not be conformed to this world, but be transformed by the renewal of their minds, that by testing they discern what is the will of God, what is good and acceptable and perfect. (from Romans 12:2 ESV)

And it is my prayer that the love of my children, (speak their names), may abound more and more, with knowledge and all discernment, so that they may be able to discern what is best and may be pure and blameless for the day of Christ, filled with the fruit of righteousness that comes through Jesus Christ, to the glory and praise of God. (from Philippians 1:9-11 ESV)

Praying for This Mama

Adonai,

There are so many times that I feel lost and overwhelmed as a parent! I want to be a good mom but often feel inadequate. There are so many hard decisions to make and difficult situations to navigate. But I know that I am not alone! Instead of turning to the world for advice and answers, let me daily abide in You and seek Your wisdom! As I draw near to You, I know You will be faithful to illuminate my path and be my compass. Teach me how to be quiet in all the busyness and chaos so that I may listen for Your voice. I trust that You will provide me with understanding and discernment. Let me cherish the wisdom You provide and lovingly apply it as I love and care for my children.

In the precious name of Jesus, I pray. Amen.

Praise Points: Praising You for the Gift of Wisdom

Lord, my heart is filled with gratitude and thanksgiving because...

- Wisdom from above is first pure, then peaceable, gentle, open to reason, full of mercy and full of fruits, impartial and sincere. (from James 3:17 ESV)
- Blessed is the one who finds wisdom and the one who gets understanding. (from Proverbs 3:13 ESV)

- You enlighten the eyes of my heart so that I may know what is the hope to which You have called me. (from Ephesians 1:18 NIV)

- The one who pleases God is given wisdom and knowledge and joy. (from Ecclesiastes 2:26 ESV)

What Do You Think? Questions for Reflection or Group Discussion

1. According to God's Word, what is wisdom?

2. How do we and our children obtain wisdom?

3. How do wisdom and intelligence differ?

4. Why does God describe wisdom and understanding as treasures?

5. Why is the fear of God cited as the beginning of wisdom?

6. What does it mean to be wise in your own eyes?

7. How can wisdom lead to salvation through faith in Jesus Christ?

Praying For Your Children to be Full of Compassion

Abba Father,

Praise be to the God and Father of our Lord Jesus Christ, the Father of compassion and the God of all comfort, who comforts us in all of our troubles, so that we can comfort those in any trouble with the comfort we ourselves receive from God (from 2 Corinthians 1:3-4 NIV). Lord, I pray that the trials that my children endure would teach them compassion and empathy and enable them to reach out to others that are in need of kindness and comfort. As one of God's chosen ones, holy and beloved, I pray that my children would daily be conformed into Your image and would cultivate compassionate hearts, kindness, meekness, and patience. May they be willing to bear the burdens of others and to walk alongside others during their time of need (from Colossians 3:12-13 ESV). Teach my children to be kind to one another and tenderhearted. May they forgive one another as God in Christ forgave us. Jehovah, enable and empower my children to administer true justice and to demonstrate mercy and compassion to one another. May they never oppress the widow or the fatherless, the foreigner or the poor (from Zechariah 7:9-10 NIV). I pray that my children would do nothing out of selfish ambition or vain conceit. Instead, I pray that my children, in humility will value others above themselves (from Philippians 2:3 NIV). Finally, may my children live

40

lives that offer sympathy, brotherly love, tender hearts, and humble minds (from 1 Peter 3:8 ESV).

In the mighty name of Jesus, I pray. Amen.

Scriptural Declarations to Pray Over Your Children

My children, (speak their names), will act justly, love mercy, and walk humbly with their God. (from Micah 6:8 NIV)

May my children, (names of your children), bear one another's burdens, and so fulfill the law of Christ. (from Galatians 6:2 ESV)

(Names of children), will rejoice with those who rejoice and weep with those who weep. (from Romans 12:15 ESV)

(Names of children), will live out a faith that is pure and undefiled before God, the Father. They will visit/care for orphans and widows in their affliction and keep themselves unstained from the world. (from James 1:27 ESV)

Praying for This Mama

Father God,

Conform me into Your image! Instill in my heart Your compassion so that I can respond to my children with love, understanding, and caring even in the most challenging and trying situations. Let me view my children through Your eyes and to gain insight into their struggles and to meet their needs with understanding and loving kindness. When I sin against my children, please be quick to convict me, Lord. Help me to admit my mistakes and to tell my kids that I am sorry when I fall short. May I provide a godly example for my children of humility and a spirit that is sensitive to the correction and guidance of the Holy Spirit.

Enable me to demonstrate compassion not only at home but also in our community. May my children witness me being the hands and feet of Jesus to the hurting, lonely, lost, and broken people of the world. Help me to welcome "interruptions" and the opportunity to be a vessel of Your love and grace to those around me, especially the children that You have entrusted into my care.

In the powerful name of Jesus, I pray. Amen.

Praise Points: Praising God for His Goodness and Mercy

Lord, I am rejoicing in hope and filled with gratitude because...

- Goodness and mercy follow me all the days of my life, and I shall dwell in the house of the Lord forever. (from Psalm 23:6 ESV)
- You are good and forgiving, abounding in steadfast love to all who call upon You. (from Psalm 86:5 ESV)
- Abundant is Your goodness, which You have stored up for those who fear You and worked for those who take refuge in You. (from Psalm 31:19 ESV)
- You are merciful and gracious; slow to anger and abounding in steadfast love. (from Psalm 103:8 ESV)
- I can draw near to the throne of grace, that I may receive mercy and find grace to help in time of need. (from Hebrews 4:16 ESV)

What Do You Think? Questions for Reflection or Group Discussion

1. What is compassion?
2. How does God show compassion to us?
3. How can God use our suffering and pain to benefit others?

4. How can our trials strengthen our faith?

5. In what ways can we demonstrate compassion to our children?

6. How can we engage our children to show compassion to others in our community?

Praying for Your Children to be Humble

Lord,

I offer thanksgiving and praise, for You are gentle and humble in heart. May my children take Your yoke upon themselves and learn from You, for this is how they will find rest for their souls. Indeed Lord, Your yoke is easy and Your burden is light (from Matthew 11:29-30 ESV)! Lord, You are good and upright! Please instruct my children in Your ways and empower them to resist pridefulness and to instead embrace humility in all things. Guide my children in what is right and teach them Your ways (from Psalm 25:8-9 NIV). The world and our flesh encourage us to seek the approval of men and to strive for accolades and acknowledgement. We can foolishly take our eyes off of You and place all our attention and focus on our accomplishments, awards, success and notoriety. Sadly, it is so easy for us to fall prey to the sin of pride. Lord, please help my children to guard against this! Your Word warns us that pride goes before destruction and a haughty spirit before a fall (from Proverbs 16:18 NIV). Lord You oppose the proud but give grace to the humble (from James 4:6 ESV). You have made it clear in Your Holy Word that the consequences of pride and a lack of humility are devastating. Lord, deliver my children from the sin of pride and cultivate in them a contrite heart that seeks You and desires to exalt and glorify You! Teach them and empower them to act justly, to love mercy, and to walk humbly with You, the Most High God! Let my children turn their eyes to You daily and abide in You, find their worth in You, and be conformed into Your image. As Your chosen people, holy and dearly loved, may my children be clothed with compassion, kindness, humility, gentleness, and patience (from Colossians 3:12 NIV). Thank You for the good work that You have begun in my children and will be faithful to bring unto completion. You are worthy to be praised!

In the name of Jesus, I pray. Amen.

Scriptural Declarations to Pray Over Your Children

My children, (speak their names), will do nothing from selfish ambition or conceit, but in humility will count others more significant than themselves. Each of them will look not only to their own interests, but also to the interests of others. (from Philippians 2:3-4 ESV)

Let all bitterness and wrath and anger and clamor and slander be put away from (names of children), along with malice. My children will be kind to one another, tenderhearted, forgiving one another, as God in Christ forgave you. (from Ephesians 4:31-32 ESV)

My children, (speak their names), will humble themselves under the mighty hand of God so that at the proper time He may exult them. (from 1 Peter 5:6 ESV)

(Names of children), will set their minds on things that are above, not on things that are here on earth. (from Colossians 3:2 ESV)

As God's chosen one's, holy and beloved, (names of children), will put on compassionate hearts, kindness, meekness, and patience. (from Colossians 3:12 ESV)

Praying for This Mama

Heavenly Father,

Keep me humble, Lord. As I learn and grow as a parent, help me guard against being stubborn and prideful. May I always have a teachable spirit and be willing to learn from my mistakes. When my children are making good choices and excelling in academics, sports, or life in general, it is easy to become prideful and to give myself all the credit and the glory. Help me to remember that You are the one who provides the wisdom and guidance I so desperately need. You are my strength and strong tower that enables me to endure trials and tribulations. You hold me in Your loving embrace when my heart breaks for my children and I cannot heal their hurts or fix a hard situation.

In the precious and mighty name of Jesus, I pray. Amen.

Praise Points: Praising God for His Sovereignty

Adonai, You are worthy of our praise! I love You and worship You because...

- You can do all things, and no purpose of Yours can be thwarted. (from Job 42:2 NIV)

- You rule over all the kingdoms of the nations. In Your hand are power and might. (from 2 Chronicles 20:6 ESV)

- With God all things are possible. (Matthew 19:26 NIV)

- From You, through You, and to You are all things. (from Romans 11:36 ESV)

- You will bring unto completion the good work that You have begun in me. (from Philippians 1:6 ESV)

What Do You Think? Questions for Reflection or Group Discussion

1. What does it mean to be prideful?

2. Why do you think God repeatedly speaks about pride in the Bible?

3. How can being prideful damage or destroy our relationship with God? With others?

4. What warning does God give about the sin of pride?

5. In what ways have you struggled with pride?

6. What does it mean to be humble?

7. How can we demonstrate humility in our lives?

Praying for Your Children to have a Servant's Heart

Abba Father,

In Your Word, You teach us that we are Your workmanship. We were created in Christ Jesus for good works (from Ephesians 2:10 ESV). Lord, I pray that each of my children will have a servant's heart that is filled with a faith that not only loves in word and speech, but also in actions and in truth (from 1 John 3:18 NIV). Enable my children to utilize the gifts and talents You have given them to bless and serve others. Create in them hearts that have an overwhelming desire to help and minister to the weak, the downtrodden and the broken-hearted. May my children quickly discern the needs in our family, church, and community and endeavor to meet those needs. Help me to find opportunities to serve and minister alongside of my children so that I may nurture and cultivate their ability to render service with a good will as to the Lord and not to man (from Ephesians 6:7 ESV) and to experience first-hand that it is more blessed to give than to receive (from Acts 20:35 NIV). We are instructed in scripture that if faith does not have works, it is dead (from James 2:17 ESV). Empower my children to have a faith that is alive and that is being lived out daily as they extend kindness, compassion, and generosity to others through their good deeds. Open the hearts of my children so they recognize that Jesus, the Son of Man, did not come to be served but to serve, and to give His life as ransom for many (from Matthew 20:28 NIV). May my children follow the example that Jesus lived out faithfully. Lord, help my children to be humble and to understand wholeheartedly that if anyone wants to be first, he must be last of all and servant of all (from Mark 9:35 ESV). Empower my children to give of themselves to others sacrificially and to love their neighbor. May my children never grow weary of doing good (from Galatians 6:9 ESV). May they love and serve others well and share what they have, for such sacrifices are pleasing to, Lord (from Hebrews 13:16 ESV)!

In the powerful name of Jesus, I pray. Amen.

Scriptural Declarations to Pray Over Your Children

As each of my children has received a gift, they will use it to serve one another, as good stewards of God's varied grace. (1 Peter 4:10 ESV)

My children, (speak their names), will help the weak and remember the words of Jesus, "It is more blessed to give than to receive." (from Acts 20:35 NIV)

My children, (speak their names), will let their lights shine before others, so that they may see Your good works and give glory to the Father who is in heaven. (from Matthew 5:16 ESV)

My children, (speak their names), will love in deed and truth. (from 1 John 3:18 ESV)

(Names of children) will only fear the Lord and serve Him faithfully with all their hearts. They will consider the great things the Lord has done for them. (from 1 Samuel 12:24 ESV)

My children, (speak their names), shall open wide their hands to their brother, to the needy and to the poor. (from Deuteronomy 15:11 ESV)

Praying for This Mama

Abba Father,

Sometimes I am just flat-out tired and exhausted! There are so many responsibilities as a parent and demands on my time. I struggle with finding balance. At times, I feel unappreciated and even resentful that I am called to make so many sacrifices as a mom. When I am feeling this way, help me to confide in You and to be willing to gain Your perspective. Remind me of Your son, Jesus, who left heaven and willingly gave His life so that we might live. May I follow His example of servanthood. Strengthen me to meet the needs of my children with a servant's heart. Teach me to have patience with my children and to respond with kindness. May I view my role as a mother as a high and noble calling that will often require me to put the needs of my children and others before my own. Enable me to extend love and kindness to my family and others as I live out my faith abiding in You.

In the precious name of Jesus, I pray. Amen.

Praise Points: Praising God for His Sacrificial Love for Us

Lord, I am rejoicing in hope and filled with gratitude because...

- Your son, Jesus, came not to be served but to serve, and to give His life as a ransom for many. (from Mark 10:45 ESV)

- You show your love for us in that while we were still sinners, Christ died for us. (from Romans 5:8 ESV)

- Everyone who calls upon the name of the Lord shall be saved. (from Acts 2:21 NIV)

- You are Lord! You have called me in righteousness and will take me by the hand and keep me. (from Isaiah 42:6-8 ESV)

- You are near to all who call upon You, to all who call on You in truth. You fulfill the desires of those who fear You. You hear our cry and save us! (from Psalm 145:18-19 NIV)

- You are in my midst, a mighty one who will save; You will rejoice over me with gladness; You will quiet me with your love and exult over me with loud singing. (from Zephaniah 3:17 ESV)

What Do You Think? Questions for Reflection or Group Discussion

1. What does it mean to have a servant's heart?
2. How do we love others in deed and truth?
3. What does God mean when He said that faith without works is dead?
4. What are some gifts that God has given you?
5. What are some gifts that God has given each of your children?
6. How can you use your God-given gifts to bless others?
7. Why is it more blessed to give than to receive?

Praying for Your Children to be Grateful

Abba Father,

May the hearts of my children abound in gratitude and overflow with thankfulness. On their best day and their worst day, may they be able to rejoice and be glad in it, for You have made each and every day (from Psalm 118:24 ESV). While living in this sinful and fallen world, my children will experience love and joy, but they will also know sadness and grief. My hope and prayer are that my children's sense of gratitude would not depend on their circumstances. Rather, may their thanks be based on Your goodness and Your steadfast love for us that endures forever (from Psalm 136:1 ESV)! May my children recognize and remember that every good and perfect gift is from above, coming down from You, the Father of Lights (from James 1:17 ESV). May they look around daily and count the blessings that You have given so freely and be grateful for not only the material provisions but also for the spiritual gifts You have given to each of them. Lord, during trials and tribulations, remind my children that for those who love You and are called according to Your purpose, You work all things together for good. Even when others come against my children and have evil intentions, You can bring good from it (from Romans 8:28 ESV). Heavenly Father, I thank You for the assured victory that is available to my children through our Lord Jesus Christ. Please enable and empower my children to rejoice always, pray continually, and give thanks in all circumstances. For this is Your will for my children (from 1 Thessalonians 5:16-18 NIV). May it be accomplished in each of their lives and may they bring You glory, honor, and praise!

In the mighty name of Jesus, I pray. Amen.

Scriptural Declarations to Pray Over Your Children

And whatever (names of children) do, in word or deed, may they do everything in the name of the Lord Jesus, giving thanks to God the Father through Him. (from Colossians 3:17 NIV)

Therefore, let (names of children), be grateful for receiving a kingdom that cannot be shaken and thus let them offer to God acceptable worship, with reverence and awe. (from Hebrews 12:28 ESV)

And let the peace of Christ rule in the hearts of my children, (speak their names). Let the Word of Christ dwell in them richly, teaching and admonishing one another in all wisdom, singing psalms and hymns and spiritual songs, with thankfulness in their hearts to God. And whatever they do, in word or deed, may my children do everything in the name of the Lord Jesus, giving thanks to the Father through Him. (from Colossians 3:15-17 ESV)

May my children, (speak their names), make a joyful noise to the Lord. May they serve the Lord with gladness and come into His presence with singing. May they know that the Lord, He is God. May my children enter His gates with thanksgiving and His courts with praise and give thanks to Him and bless His name! For the Lord is good; His steadfast love endures forever, and His faithfulness to all generations. (from Psalm 100: 1-5 ESV)

Praying for This Mama

Father God,

If I am being honest, there are times as a parent when I feel frustrated, disappointed, unappreciated, overwhelmed, and broken-hearted. I confess that during these times it is easier to complain and to be angry with You. Sometimes I even blame You for my circumstance. Forgive me, Heavenly Father! The desire of my heart is that during the greatest storms of my life, I would run to You and not away from You. May I be filled with gratitude for You, because You are the same yesterday, today, and forever. You are the Unchanging One. Your love for me is everlasting and steadfast − that never changes! Your promises are trustworthy! May the overflow of my heart be praise and thanksgiving that spills out in worship of You even in the most difficult of days.

In the precious name of Jesus, I pray. Amen.

Praise Points: Praising God for the Good Gifts He Gives

Lord, I come to you with thanksgiving and praise because...

- Every good gift and every perfect gift are from above, coming down from the Father of lights with whom there is no variation or shadow due to change. (from James 1:17 ESV)
- The wages of sin are death, but the free gift of God is eternal life in Christ Jesus our Lord. (from Romans 12:6 ESV)
- For by grace you have been saved through faith. And this is not your own doing, it is the gift of God. (from Ephesians 2:8 ESV)
- Each of us (followers of Jesus) is given the manifestation of the Spirit for the common good. For to one is given through the Spirit the utterance of wisdom, and to another the utterance of knowledge according to the same Spirit, to another

faith by the same Spirit, to another gifts of healing by the one Spirit, to another the working of miracles, to another prophecy, to another the ability to distinguish between spirits, to another various kinds of tongues, to another interpretation of tongues. All of these are empowered by the one and the same Holy Spirit, who apportions to each one individually as He wills. (from 1 Corinthians 12:7-11 ESV)

What Do You Think? Questions for Reflection or Group Discussion

1. What is gratitude?

2. What are you most grateful for?

3. Can you list 10 of the good gifts that God has given you?

4. What is the greatest of all gifts given by God?

5. Think of times in your life that you were ungrateful. Why do you think you struggled with being thankful in these circumstances?

6. How can gratitude aid in strengthening our faith?

7. What are the spiritual gifts that God has given to you? How can you use them to bless and encourage others?

Praying for Your Children to be Generous

Father God,

May my children lovingly desire to share their time, talents, and wealth with others that are in need. Open their eyes so they are aware and their hearts so they are sensitive to those that are hurting, downtrodden, despairing, abused, or in crisis. May they employ the unique gifts and talents that You have given them and use them freely to minister to others and bless them. May they honor Your will by doing good, being rich in good works, being generous and ready to share the resources You have provided, for such sacrifices are pleasing to You Lord (from 1 Timothy 6:18 ESV and Hebrews 13:16 ESV). Empower my children to incline their hearts to Your testimonies, and not to selfish gains (from Psalm 119:36 ESV). Help them to resist any urges to be selfish, greedy, or uncharitable. Guard them also from a judgmental attitude. Instead, may their lights shine brightly in the darkness as they reach out to the lost and broken with kindness and generosity. May they freely share with others what You have so lovingly given to them. Enable my children to overflow with Your love and grace so that they may not love in word or talk but in deed and in truth (1 John 3:18 ESV).

In the precious name of Jesus, I pray. Amen.

Scriptural Declarations to Pray Over Your Children

And God is able to make all grace abound in my children, (speak their names), so that having all sufficiency in all things at all times, they may abound in every good work. (from 2 Corinthians 9:8 ESV)

My children, (speak their names), will help the weak and remember the words of the Lord Jesus, how He Himself said, "It is more blessed to give than to receive." (from Acts 20:35 NIV)

(Names of children), will bear one another's burdens, and so fulfill the law of Christ. (from Galatians 6:2 ESV)

May (names of children) judge not, and they will not be judged; condemn not, and they will not be condemned; forgive, and they will be forgiven; give, and it will be given to them. Good measure, pressed down, shaken together, running over, will be poured into your lap. For with the measure you use, it will be measured to you. (from Luke 6:37-38 NIV)

Praying for This Mama

Abba Father,

Let me give freely to my children my love, my understanding, and my time. Destroy any selfish motives or tendencies that exist in me and help me to meet their needs consistently and extend grace daily. Allow me to demonstrate patience, kindness, and forgiveness to my children even when it is not easy to do so. May I joyfully invest in them and train them in your ways. Let me live out a life of generosity and giving out of love that points my children to You and strengthens their faith.

In the precious name of Jesus, I pray. Amen.

Praise Points: Praising God for His Enduring Love

Adonai, you are worthy of our praise! I love You and worship You because...

- Your steadfast love endures forever! (from Psalm 118:1 ESV)

- You have loved me with an everlasting love. You have drawn me with unfailing kindness. (from Jeremiah 31:3 NIV)

- Neither death nor life, neither angels nor demons, neither the present nor the future, nor any powers, neither height nor depth, nor anything else in all creation, will be able to separate us from the love of God that is in Christ Jesus our Lord. (from Romans 8:38-39 NIV)

- You are the same yesterday, today, and forever! (from Hebrews 13:8 ESV)

What Do You Think? Questions for Reflection or Group Discussion

1. What is generosity?

2. What are some ways that you have been generous in the past?

3. When and in what ways have you struggled with being generous to others? Have you ever worried that if you are obedient to the Lord in your giving that you might not have enough for yourself or your family?

4. Have you ever gone without something so that someone else was provided for? What was that like for you?

5. How aware and sensitive are you to the needs of those around you?

6. What does it mean to be a good steward with the income and resources that God provides for us?

7. What does it mean to be a good steward with our time and talents?

Praying for Your Children to Speak Life

Heavenly Father,

Words are important! You spoke the world into existence with Your holy utterances. You tell us that Your Word is alive and active. There is an awesome power in Your words, Lord! And You also instruct us that the words that we speak matter. My prayer is that daily my children will choose to speak life - for death and life are in the power of the tongue (from Proverbs 18:21 ESV). Lord, set a guard over the mouths of my children and keep watch over the doors of their lips (from Psalm 141:3 NIV). May my children use their words to encourage, comfort, bring healing and proclaim truth. Help them to listen carefully to others and to be thoughtful before speaking. May they always choose words that are respectful and that convey and speak the truth in love (from Ephesians 4:15 ESV). In the Gospel of Matthew, You warn us that on the day of judgement, we will all give an account for every careless word we speak (from Matthew 12:36-37 ESV). Help my children to be careful in their speech and to resist the temptation to engage in gossip or to spread falsehoods about others. Rather than complaining, let them offer words of thanksgiving and gratitude for the many blessings in their lives. Instill in them a love of the truth and give them the strength and courage to tell the truth and avoid lies. If they do tell lies or are deceitful, make them so uncomfortable that they cannot find peace or relief until they are willing to confess and be truthful about the situation at hand. Father God, let the words of my children's mouths and the meditation of their hearts be acceptable in Your sight (from Psalm 19:14 ESV)! Teach and empower them to have a gentle tongue that gives soft answers (from Proverbs 15:1-4 ESV). Let their speech always be gracious, seasoned with salt, so that they may know how they ought to answer each person (Colossians 4:6 ESV). May both the spoken and written words of my children be life-giving and bring You honor and glory. May they daily give thanks and sing Your praises!

In the mighty and matchless name of Jesus, I pray. Amen.

Scriptural Declarations to Pray Over Your Children

May my children, (speak their names), open their mouths with wisdom, and may the teaching of kindness be on their tongues. (from Proverbs 31:26 ESV)

May my children, (speak their names), have the tongue of the wise that brings healing. (from Proverbs 12:18 NIV)

Let there be no filthiness, foolish talk, or crude joking uttered by (names of children), but instead let there be thanksgiving. (from Ephesians 5:4 ESV)

Speaking the truth in love, (names of children) are to grow up in every way into Him who is the head, into Christ. (from Ephesians 4:15 ESV)

Praying for This Mama

Adonai,

Sometimes I speak before I think! In anger and frustration, I can utter words that are critical, harsh, and hurtful to my children. When that happens, help me to quickly be convicted and to ask Your forgiveness and that of my children. My sincere hope and prayer is that You will help me to guard my mouth and to carefully choose my words. May my words offer love, encouragement, and wisdom to my children. Help me to daily speak life, light, and truth over my kids! As I read your God-breathed, holy, inspired words in scripture, may it be rooted in my spirit and overflow into my speech. Let me proclaim Your truths and promises over my children and speak blessings upon them.

In the mighty name of Jesus, I pray. Amen.

Praise Points: Praising God for Comforting Us

Abba Father, I come to You with thanksgiving in my heart because...

- You are the Father of mercies and God of all comfort, who comforts us in all our affliction, so that we may be able to comfort those who are in any affliction. (from 2 Corinthians 1:3-4 ESV)
- Even though I walk through the valley of the shadow of death, I will fear no evil, for You are with me; Your rod and staff, they comfort me. (from Psalm 23:4 ESV)
- Your steadfast love comforts me according to Your promises. (from Psalm 119:76 ESV)
- This is my comfort in my affliction, that Your promise gives me life. (from Psalm 119:50 ESV)
- Blessed are those that mourn, for they shall be comforted. (from Matthew 5:4 NIV)
- You are near to the brokenhearted and save the crushed in spirit. (from Psalm 34:18 ESV)
- You heal the brokenhearted and bind up their wounds. (from Psalm 147:3 NIV)

What Do You Think? Questions for Reflection or Group Discussion

1. How did God bring the world into existence? (Look in Genesis if you are unsure)

2. What does God reveal to us about His Word?

3. What does God mean when He says that our tongues have the power of death and life?

4. How can we speak words that are life-giving to our children and to others?

5. What does it mean to set a guard over our mouths?

6. Do you ever struggle with gossip? How can a believer avoid engaging in gossip?

7. Why is it important that we pray God's words/scriptures over our children?

Praying for Your Children to have a Sound Mind

Adonai,

As my children draw near to You, I pray that You would cultivate in them a sound mind. Deliver them from any lies or false beliefs from the enemy. May these deceptions that bring death and devastation be exposed, uprooted, and destroyed and replaced with Your loving and powerful truths! Enable my children to take every thought captive and make it obedient to You, Lord (from 2 Corinthians 10:5 NIV). Strengthen them, Adonai, so that they will not conform to the pattern of this world, but instead be transformed by the renewing of their minds. Thus, they will be empowered to test and approve what your good, pleasing, and perfect will is for them (from Romans 12:2 NIV). In your Word, You promise to keep in perfect peace those whose minds are stayed on You and who place their trust in You (from Isaiah 26:3 ESV). Lord, I praise You that You can bring a lasting peace to the minds and spirits of my children. I overflow with gratitude that You are able to deliver my children and free them from depression, anxiety, self-destructive thoughts, hatred towards self or others, violent thoughts, lustful thoughts and obsessions. I pray that my children would have stable and sound minds that do not succumb to mental illnesses or to the lies of the world or the enemy. Enable them to have clarity of thought, to focus, and to be able to comprehend, retain, and apply the things they learn. Help them to understand that the things they watch, read, listen to, and speak will influence their thoughts and their mind. Let them continually turn their thoughts to whatever is true, whatever is honorable, whatever is just, whatever is pure, whatever is lovely, and whatever is commendable. If there is anything of excellence and worthy of praise, may they think on these things (Philippians 4:8 ESV). Renew their minds continually Lord! May the words of their mouth adore you and the meditation of their hearts be acceptable in your sight, O Lord, our rock and redeemer (from Psalm 19:14 ESV). I shout hallelujah because in You, my children can be overcomers!

In the mighty name of Jesus, I pray. Amen.

Scriptural Declarations to Pray Over Your Children

My children, (speak their names), will set their minds on things that are above, not on things that are on earth. (from Colossians 3:2 ESV)

(Names of children), will keep their hearts with all vigilance, for from it flows the springs of life. (from Proverbs 4:23 ESV)

My children, (speak their names), will not be anxious about anything, but will let their requests be known to God by prayer and supplication with thanksgiving. And the peace of God, which surpasses all understanding, will guard their hearts and minds in Christ Jesus. (from Philippians 4:6-7 ESV)

My children, (speak their names), will not be conformed to this world, instead they will be transformed by the renewing of their minds, that by testing they will discern what is the will of God, what is good and acceptable and perfect. (from Romans 12:2 ESV)

Praying for This Mama

Heavenly Father,

When I give into the busyness of the world and do not take the time to abide in You, I am overcome by anxiety and plagued by doubt! During these times, there is no balance and I become overwhelmed and discouraged. All my fears and insecurities consume my thoughts and my emotions are such a rollercoaster! I know this keeps me from being the mom that I want to be! However, I know that I do not have to live a life that is marked repeatedly by those destructive thoughts and patterns. Instead, my desire is to daily abide in You and hold my thoughts captive! With Your help, I can reclaim any territory in my life that has been surrendered to the enemy of my soul. Your light exposes the lies and lovingly replaces them with Your truth. Help me to walk in the freedom that You secured for me at Calvary with the shed blood of Your son, Jesus. Through you, I can be an overcomer. May I always remember my identity in Christ and allow my mind to daily be renewed and transformed! Create in me a sound mind that is at peace and is empowered to use sound judgement, discernment, and wisdom in parenting my children.

In the mighty and precious name of Jesus, I pray. Amen.

Praise Points: Praising God for Discernment and Understanding

Abba, I praise and worship you because...

- The Word of God is living and active, sharper than any two-edged sword, piercing to the division of soul and of spirit, of joints and of marrow, and discerning the thoughts & intentions of the heart. (from Hebrews 4:12 ESV)

- If we receive Your words and treasure up Your commandments, make our ears attentive to wisdom and incline our hearts to understanding... then we will understand the fear of the Lord and find the knowledge of God. (from Proverbs 2:1-2, 5 ESV)

- When the Spirit of truth comes, He will guide us into all truth. (from John 16:13 ESV)

- No eye has seen, nor ear heard, nor the heart of man imagined, what You have prepared for those of us who love You – these things You have revealed to us through Your Spirit. (from 1 Corinthians 2:9-10 ESV)

What Do You Think? Questions for Reflection or Group Discussion

1. What does it mean to hold your thoughts captive?

2. Why is it important to think on things that are true, honorable, just, pure, lovely, and commendable?

3. How can tv, movies, magazines, books, music, the internet, and social media impact our thoughts and our mental health?

4. What does it mean to renew our minds?

5. How can reading the Bible help us in dealing with anxieties, insecurities, and depression?

6. Have you believed any lies of the enemy? How can you identify them and break down any strongholds they have created in your life?

7. How does praying the promises of God help us in cultivating healthy minds and emotions in ourselves and our children?

8. What are some of your favorite promises found in the Bible?

Praying for Your Children to Care for Their Bodies

Adonai,

Your Word tells us that we are fearfully and wonderfully made! May my children rejoice in the fact that You created them and know in their souls that Your works are wonderful (from Psalm 139:14 NIV). Lord, You lovingly knit each of us together in the wombs of our mothers (from Psalm 139:13 NIV). We are Your image bearers and are made in Your likeness (from Genesis 1:26 NIV). May my children recognize that their bodies are a home for their spirit, and when they become followers of Jesus Christ and are born again, their bodies become a temple in which Your Holy Spirit dwells! May they understand that their bodies and their lives are not their own as they were bought at a price. May the choices that they make regarding the care and conduct of their body be glorifying to You (from 1 Corinthians 6:19-20 ESV). Instill in them a love and respect for their bodies. May they crave nutritional food that nourishes and heals them. Help them to maintain a balanced diet and to use self-control when eating. Guard my children, Lord, and protect them from eating disorders and an unhealthy relationship with food. Help my children to understand the importance of being physically active to maintain their health. Grant them the energy and motivation to exercise regularly. May they also understand the importance of good personal hygiene and cleanliness and maintain their bodies in this way. Because my children acknowledge that their bodies are a gift from You, Lord, may they never pollute or damage themselves through the abuse of drugs and never become a prisoner to addiction. Strengthen my children and empower them to love themselves and their body and to see the beauty that You placed in them. Protect them from thoughts of self-harm and suicide and let them run to You, their refuge and strong tower, when they are suffering and in need of comfort and consoling. Place in their hearts a desire to use their bodies in service to You through ministry and good works. May they present their bodies as living sacrifices, holy and acceptable to You, Lord, and thus worship and glorify You (from Romans 12:1 ESV)!

In the precious name of Jesus, I pray. Amen.

Scriptural Declarations to Pray for Your Children

The flesh and hearts of my children, (speak their names), may fail, but God is the strength of their hearts and their portion forever. (from Psalm 73:26 ESV)

May my children, (speak their names), not be wise in their own eyes; may they fear the Lord and shun evil. This will bring health to their bodies and nourishment to their bones. (from Proverbs 3:7-8 NIV)

May my children, (speak their names), flee from sexual immorality. Every other sin a person commits is outside the body, but the sexually immoral person sins against his own body. (from 1 Corinthians 6:18 ESV)

(Names of children), do not fear those who kill the body but cannot kill the soul. Rather fear Him who can destroy both soul and body in hell. (from Matthew 10:28 ESV)

The eye is the lamp of the body. May the eyes of my children, (speak their names), be healthy, so their whole bodies will be full of light. (from Matthew 6:22 ESV)

Praying for This Mama

Heavenly Father,

I struggle with being grateful for my body. Often, I fall prey to comparing my looks and my weight to other women on social media and in day-to-day life. I tend to be too critical of myself and sometimes make negative comments about my appearance. Remind me, Lord, that I am fearfully and wonderfully made! You knit me together in my mother's womb and You know every detail about me. Help me to be kind to myself and to love and appreciate my body. Thank you, Lord that my body has been made for life-giving and nurturing. I have had so many opportunities to extend your love with hands that reach out to help others. You tell me in your Word that my body is a temple for the Holy Spirit that dwells in me. Show me how to truly love and care for my body and to be grateful for it. Place in me the desire to eat nourishing and healthy foods and to get ample exercise. Empower me to be a positive role model to my children in leading a healthy lifestyle and making self-care a priority. Let me delight in who You created me to be... mind, body, and spirit!

In the powerful name of Jesus, I pray. Amen.

Praise Points: Praising God for Lovingly Creating Us

Lord, my heart is filled with gratitude and thanksgiving because...

- Our bodies become a temple of the Holy Spirit when we put our faith in You, Lord! (from 1 Corinthians 6:19 ESV)
- Before You formed me in the womb, You knew me. (from Jeremiah 1:5 NIV)
- You formed my inward parts; You knitted me together in my mother's womb... I am fearfully and wonderfully made. Wonderful are Your works; my soul knows it very well. (from Psalm 139:13-14 ESV)

- Your sacrifice and atonement for our sins makes it so that our bodies can be a living sacrifice, holy and acceptable to You. (from Romans 12:1 ESV)

- You created us in Your own image. (from Genesis 1:27 NIV)

- The Spirit of Him who raised Jesus from the dead dwells in me, He who raised Christ Jesus from the dead will also give life to my mortal body through his Spirit who dwells in me. (from Romans 8:11 ESV)

What Do You Think? Questions for Reflection or Group Discussion

1. What does it mean to be an image bearer of God?

2. What kind of responsibilities come with being an image bearer? How can our behavior impact people who have not yet placed their faith in Jesus?

3. What did God mean when He referred to the bodies of believers as being a temple for the Holy Spirit?

4. In what ways have you been ungrateful for your body or been unkind to it?

5. Think of 5 things that you like and/or appreciate about your body.

6. How can you help your children in developing a healthy body image?

7. What are practical steps that you can take to care for and nourish your body?

8. How can you demonstrate love and appreciation for your body through your speech/words?

Praying for Your Children to have Freedom from Fear

Heavenly Father,

I lift up my children to You and pray that they will have freedom from fear and that their faith will preside in their hearts. May they rest in the assurance that You are their protector! Let my children place their trust in You daily and know that You are their rock, their fortress, and their deliverer (from Psalm 18:2 NIV). I praise You Lord that You go before each of my children and You have promised that You will never leave or forsake them (from Deuteronomy 31:6 NIV). You will guard my children against the evil one (from 2 Thessalonians 3:3 ESV), for You are their shield, the horn of their salvation, and their stronghold (from Psalm 18:2 ESV). May each of my children receive the peace that You have promised and rest in it. Let not their hearts be troubled or afraid (from John 14:27 ESV) for You have not given us a spirit of fear! Lord, Your Spirit does not make us timid, instead it gives us power, love, and self-discipline (from 2 Timothy 1:7 NIV). My children will not be dismayed or overcome by fear, for You are their God. You will strengthen them, help them, and uphold them with Your righteous right hand (from Isaiah 41:10 ESV). You have instructed us not to be anxious about anything! Instead, by prayer and petition, with thanksgiving, we are to present our requests to You, and the peace of God, which transcends all understanding, will guard our hearts and minds (Philippians 4:6-7

NIV). May this be the reality in the lives of each of my children! May the seeds of my children's faith grow abundantly. Let them drink deeply of Your living waters and find strength in your light and love. As they abide in You daily, may their faith be deeply rooted and bear the fruit of Your Holy Spirit! May their faith be ever increasing and enduring. For where faith abounds there is no allowance for worries or worldly fear. May any strongholds of fear that have been cultivated in my children be destroyed and that territory reclaimed for Your glory, Lord! I boldly declare that my children will not be shaken, but instead put their hope and trust in You daily - for You are their light and salvation, whom shall they fear? You are their stronghold, of whom shall they be afraid? (from Psalm 27:1 NIV)

In the mighty and powerful name of Jesus, I pray. Amen.

Scriptural Declarations to Pray Over Your Children

May the hearts of (names of children) not be troubled, neither let them be afraid. (from John 14:27 ESV)

May (names of children) fear not, for You Lord are with them. Let them not be dismayed, for You are their God. You will strengthen them, You will help them, You will uphold (names of children) with Your righteous right hand. (from Isaiah 41:10 ESV)

The Lord is (names of children) light and salvation; whom shall they fear? The Lord is the stronghold of their lives, of whom shall they be afraid? (from Psalm 27:1 NIV)

When my children, (names of children), are afraid, they will put their trust in You. (from Psalm 56:3 NIV)

The Lord is (names of children) rock, fortress and deliverer in whom they will take refuge. The Lord is their shield, the horn of their salvation, their stronghold. (from Psalm 18:2 ESV)

My children, (speak their names,) will say to the Lord, "My refuge and my fortress, my God, in whom I trust." (from Psalm 91:2 ESV)

Praying for This Mama

Lord,

My worries and concerns for my children are many! Help me to not be overwhelmed and encompassed by my fears. But instead, help me to shape them into prayers. Let me leave my fears at Your cross and exchange them daily for Your peace. May I wholeheartedly put my hope and trust in You and You alone. Let me abide in Your loving care and trust in Your promise that You will never leave me or forsake me. Remind me that I don't have to rely on my own strength to be a good mom, but instead be renewed and strengthened by your Holy Spirit! Thank you, Lord that You go before me and You've got my back! You are a faithful and covenant God. It is comforting to know that You will guide me in this journey of being a parent. I know You love my kids even more than I do! Help me to love, nurture and train the children You have entrusted into my care. Lord, replace my fear with faith as I trust in You.

In the mighty name of Jesus, I pray. Amen.

Praise Points: Praising God for His Protection

Lord, today I come into Your presence with praise and thanksgiving! I am grateful that...

- You are my hiding place; You will protect me from trouble and surround me with songs of deliverance. (from Psalm 32:7 NIV)
- You are my rock and my fortress and my deliverer. (from Psalm 18:2 ESV)

- You, Lord God, go with me. You will never leave nor forsake me. (from Deuteronomy 31:6 NIV)

- No weapon forged against me will prevail, and I will refute every tongue that accuses me. This is the heritage of the servants of the Lord. (from Isaiah 54:17 NIV)

- You will guard me against the evil one. (from 2 Thessalonians 3:3 ESV)

- You make your saving help my shield, and Your right hand sustains me. (from Psalm 18:35 NIV)

- You will fight for me Lord! I need only be still. (from Exodus 14:14 NIV)

- You are at my right hand; I will not be shaken. I keep my eyes always on the Lord. (from Psalm 16:8 NIV)

What Do You Think? Questions for Reflection or Group Discussion

1. The Lord tells us in His Word that He has not given us a spirit of fear. What has He given us instead?

2. The Lord has instructed us to be anxious for nothing. What does He tell us to do instead?

3. What are your biggest fears in life? What are your greatest worries about your children?

4. How does reading your Bible and praying scripture over your children help with fear?

5. Many times, throughout the Bible, God commanded us to not fear. Why do you think He was so adamant about this?

Praying for Healthy Family Relationships

Yahweh,

May our family be established and built upon Jesus Christ, our rock and cornerstone. I pray Your nurturing and protection over these God-ordained relationships between parents and children and between siblings. Help us to cultivate a home that is a place of peace, harmony, and refuge where our children feel safe, secure, nurtured, and loved. Facilitate open and honest communication that is respectful and speaks the truth in love. May each member of our family be able to express their feelings freely and feel valued and heard. Enable our children to ask for help and to reach out when they are struggling. Adonai, help us to guard against misunderstandings and not allow divisions to take root. May we never provide an opportunity for the enemy to gain a stronghold in our family through unforgiveness, bitterness, or jealousy. Help us to navigate conflict among each other with wisdom, discernment, and compassion. Teach us how to truly listen and to lend understanding and support to each other even in the most difficult and stressful situations. When we do sin against each other and cause hurt, disappointment, or a breach of trust, help us to forgive one another and bridge the gap. Your Word instructs us to bear with one another, and if one has a complaint against another, forgiving each other; as the Lord has forgiven you, so you also must forgive (from Colossians 3:13 ESV). Establish in the hearts of my children the desire to honor their parents and to keep their father's commandments and not forsake their mother's teaching (from Exodus 20:12 NIV and Proverbs 6:20 NIV). Strengthen our family bonds as we grow together, learn, love, and laugh together. Help us to value family time and to enjoy the company of each other. May we establish meaningful family traditions that are honoring to You and create cherished memories. My desire is that we grow in faith together and find ways to serve and minister as a family. Empower us to leave a powerful legacy of love that lasts for many generations to come. May we be devoted to one another in love and honor one another above ourselves (Romans 12:10 NIV).

In the powerful name of Jesus, I pray. Amen.

Scriptural Declarations to Pray Over Your Children

I appeal to you, (names of children), brothers and sisters, in the name of the Lord Jesus Christ, that all of You agree in what You would say and that there be no divisions among You, but that You be perfectly united in mind and thought. (from 1 Corinthians 1:10 ESV)

May (names of children), be like-minded, be sympathetic, love one another, be compassionate, and humble. (from 1 Peter 3:8 NIV)

(Names of children), do to others as you would have them do to you. (Luke 6:31 NIV)

Praying for This Mama

Abba Father,

Thank You, Lord that You have entrusted my children into my care. Being their mom is a precious and noble calling! May You empower me to love and care for my children in a way that nourishes our bond and strengthens our family. Help me to build our home and our family with Jesus as our foundation and cornerstone. May Your Holy Spirit enable me to create a home environment that is marked by Your peace and is a refuge. Help my words to be gentle and seasoned with grace. Give me the wisdom needed to cultivate trust and respect among our family members. May our home be furnished with compassion and kindness and adorned with joy and laughter! Let gratitude and contentment grow readily in our hearts as we learn to cherish the gift of family. May my soul magnify the Lord and point my children to You!

In the precious name of Jesus, I pray. Amen.

Praise Points: Praising God for Adopting Us into His Family

Abba Father, my heart is filled with gratitude and thanksgiving because...

- You predestined us for adoption as sons through Jesus Christ. (from Ephesians 1:5 ESV)

- To all who did receive Him, who believed in His name, He gave the right to become children of God. (from John 1:12 ESV)

- In Christ Jesus we are all sons of God, through faith. (from Galatians 3:26 ESV)

- We may become blameless and innocent, children of God without blemish in the midst of a crooked and twisted generation, among whom we shine as lights in the world. (from Philippians 2:15 ESV)

What Do You Think? Questions for Reflection or Group Discussion

1. How can you teach your children to communicate with their siblings and parents in a God-honoring way?

2. How can we encourage our kids to speak life-giving words to family members?

3. How can reading the Bible and memorizing Scriptures help your family in building healthy relationships with one another?

4. What does the Bible say about handling conflict? How can we apply that in our family and home?

5. What kind of traditions have you established in your family to strengthen your bond with each other?

6. How do you encourage forgiveness and extending grace in your family?

7. How do you think praying together regularly as a family can help your family?

Praying for Your Children to have Godly Friends & Mentors

Heavenly Father,

My hope and my prayer are that each of my children will be good and faithful friends to others. Let them be the kind of friend that sticks closer than a brother (from Proverbs 18:24 NIV)! May they endeavor to be thoughtful, understanding and extend kindness. Show them how to have healthy boundaries with friends and to not manipulate others or allow themselves to be manipulated. Strengthen them so that they do not compromise their faith or values to be liked and accepted by others. Give them wisdom and discernment as they make friends and invest in these relationships with their peers. Your Word instructs us that bad company ruins good morals and that whoever walks with the wise becomes wise, but the companion of fools will suffer harm (from 1 Corinthians 15:33 ESV and Proverbs 13:20 ESV). May their friendships that develop be honoring and glorifying to You. I pray that their closest companions and deepest friendships be with children/teens that love the Lord so that they may grow together in faith and help each other to resist the temptation to sin. May they provide accountability for each other and share the truth in love. Lord, please remove from the lives of my children any friends that are a bad influence on them and would lead them away from You or turn the heart of that child or teen toward You and conform them into Your image. Lord, may my children live out in their friendships the counsel provided in the book of Colossians, that as God's chosen people, holy and dearly loved, they will clothe themselves with compassion, kindness, humility, gentleness, and patience. May they bear with each other and forgive one another when they have grievances. Show them how to forgive one another as You, the Lord, have forgiven them. And over all these virtues, may they put on love, which binds them together in perfect unity (from Colossians 3:12-14 NIV).

Lord, I also come to You requesting that You provide many godly mentors for my children throughout their childhood and teen years. Place in their lives trusted role models who wholeheartedly love the Lord and have a desire to teach and mentor children/teens/young adults. May they live out their faith before my children and serve as powerful role models, displaying godly attributes and the fruit of the spirit. Let them be a source of wisdom, support, and encouragement in helping my children to nurture and grow their faith and to find their identity in Christ. In the book of Hebrews, You remind us to remember our leaders who speak the Word of God to us. Lord, You invite us to consider the outcome of their way of life and to imitate it (from Hebrews 13:7 ESV). Lord, I thank you and praise You for the provision of those types of leaders/mentors to encourage my children in their faith walk.

In the precious name of Jesus, I pray. Amen.

Scriptural Declarations to Pray Over Your Children

I pray that (names of children) will not make friends with a hot-tempered person, and that they will not associate with one easily angered, or they may learn their ways and get themselves ensnared. (from Proverbs 22:24-25 NIV)

May (names of children) not be deceived, because bad company ruins good morals. (1 Corinthians 15:33 ESV)

May my children, (speak their names), walk with the wise and thus become wise and avoid becoming the companion of fools and suffering harm. (from Proverbs 13:20 ESV)

Praying for This Mama

Father God,

Thank You for the many blessings on our family and for Your generous provision. You are so faithful to meet our needs! Lord, as a mom I can sometimes feel lonely and long for deep friendships with women that are in the same season of life as I am. Please provide opportunities for me to cultivate godly friendships that help me to grow in my faith and encourage me in my role as a mom. Help me to be a good friend who is thoughtful, dependable, listens well, encourages, demonstrates kindness, and extends grace. May these relationships be healthy and God-honoring and serve as a good example to my children.

In the matchless name of Jesus, I pray. Amen.

Praise Points: Praising the Lord for Godly Friendships

Abba Father, I come to You with thanksgiving because...

- If we walk in the light, as He is in the light, we have fellowship with one another, and the blood of Jesus His Son cleanses us from all sin. (from 1 John 1:7 ESV)
- Iron sharpens iron, and one man sharpens another. (from Proverbs 27:17 ESV)

- Where two or three are gathered in My name, there am I among them. (from Matthew 18:20 NIV)

- We may be mutually encouraged by each other's faith, both yours and mine. (from Romans 1:12 ESV)

- Their hearts may be encouraged, being knit together in love, to reach all the riches of full assurance of understanding and the knowledge of God's mystery, which is Christ. (from Colossians 2:2 ESV)

What Do You Think? Questions for Reflection or Group Discussion

1. What qualities do you think are important for a friend to have?

2. Can you think of friendships that have helped you to be a better person? What was it about those friendships that were encouraging and edifying to you?

3. What are some of your most funny and fond friendship memories?

4. What is the kindest, most meaningful thing a friend has ever done for you?

5. How can we teach our children to be a good friend to others?

6. How do you think praying scriptures over your children may help with having discernment and wisdom in parenting? How can it help when they are being negatively impacted or influenced by a friend or group of friends?

Praying Protection Over Your Children

Heavenly Father,

I praise you, Lord, that You are the protector and deliverer of my children! My heart finds comfort knowing that You are their hiding place. You will protect my children from trouble and surround them with songs of deliverance (from Psalm 32:7 NIV). Please establish a hedge of protection around each of my children. Protect them from illnesses/disease, accidents, and injuries. I pray You would strengthen and sustain their bodies and that their immune systems would be strong and work the way you designed them to. Give them each the gift of wisdom and discernment so they can make good choices and not place themselves in dangerous situations or take unnecessary risks. Help them to perceive when there is danger, or when someone wishes to do them harm. When they discern that that they are in trouble, may they immediately call on Your name, for You are their refuge and their shield. May they always put their hope in You and Your Word (from Psalm 119:114 NIV). Lord God, safeguard their spirits, minds/emotions, and bodies. Protect them from physical, sexual, and emotional abuse and from anyone that has evil intentions. Holy Spirit, daily prompt my children to put on the whole armor of God, that they may be able to stand against the schemes of the devil (from Ephesians 6:11 ESV). May they be able to discern false teachers and deceptions and be able to counter those by standing on the truths of Your Word. I am grateful Lord that as my children serve You and navigate their way in this world, You will go before them and be their rear guard (from Isaiah 52:12 NIV). My children never need to fear, for You Lord are a shield around them, their glory, the one who lifts their head high (from Psalm 3:3 NIV)!

In the mighty name of Jesus, I pray. Amen.

Scriptural Declarations to Pray Over Your Children

The name of the Lord is a fortified tower; (names of children) will run into it and be safe. (from Proverbs 18:10 NIV)

Be strong and courageous, (names of children). Do not be afraid or terrified because of them, for the Lord Your God goes with You; He will never leave or forsake you. (from Deuteronomy 31:6 NIV)

The Lord will fight for (names of children); they need only be still. (from Exodus 14:14 NIV)

Whoever dwells in the shelter of the Most High will rest in the shadow of the Almighty. (Names of children) will say of the Lord, "He is my refuge and my fortress, My God, in whom I trust." (from Psalm 91:1-2 NIV)

In peace, (names of children) will lie down and sleep; for You alone, Lord, make them dwell in safety. (Psalm 4:8 ESV)

Praying for This Mama

Heavenly Father,

I cannot even begin to count the worries and fears that have occupied my thoughts regarding the safety and well-being of my children! While part of my job is to care for my children and to keep them safe and secure, I am unable to protect them from everything. I want to be attentive to valid concerns, but I do not want to be consumed by worry and immobilized by fear! Help me to shape my fears into prayers and not carry around those burdens. Enable me to discern when there is a real threat or danger to my children and give me wisdom on how to best handle it. Let my children see me going to Your throne regularly, exchanging my worries for Your peace. May they see me running to You, my strong tower and enjoying the refuge that You provide. Let my faith extinguish my fears and provide me with the assurance of Your protection and provision for my children. You are mighty to save!

In the blessed name of Jesus, I pray. Amen.

Praise Points: Praising God for Being our Refuge

Adonai, you are worthy of our praise! I love You and worship You because...

- I can call upon You and I am saved from my enemies. You are my rock in whom I take refuge. You are my shield and the horn of my salvation, my stronghold and my refuge. You are my Savior. (from 2 Samuel 22:3-4 ESV)

- You are my refuge and my shield; I have put my hope in Your Word. (from Psalm 119:114 NIV)

- You will cover me with your pinions, and under your wings I will find refuge. (from Psalm 91:4 ESV)

- The name of the Lord is a fortified tower; the righteous run to it and are safe. (from Proverbs 18:10 NIV)

- You are our refuge and strength, and ever-present help in trouble. (from Psalm 46:1 NIV)

- You are my refuge and my fortress, my God in whom I trust. (from Psalm 91:2 ESV)

What Do You Think? Questions for Reflection and Group Discussion

1. What are your biggest fears concerning your children?

2. Have you ever made a parenting decision out of fear? How do your fears impact your parenting?

3. What lies of the enemy are you believing that cause or contribute to your fears?

4. How do you think praying Scripture can help you find freedom from your parenting fears?

5. Why is it important to pray protection over your children (but not live in fear)?

6. In what ways has the Lord protected you or been a refuge to you?

7. How has God made you feel safe and brought you peace?

THE MOST IMPORTANT PRAYER YOU CAN EVER PRAY!

The most important prayer that you can ever pray for your children or for any loved one is that they would find salvation in our Lord Jesus Christ! The Word of God (the Bible) tells us that everyone has sinned and falls short of the glory of God. That sin has separated each of us from God and sentenced us to death. That is really bad news! No one wants a death sentence. But that does not need to be the end of my story, or your story, or anyone else's story. There is good news! The Word of God proclaims that our one true hope, our only hope, is found in Jesus!

Our Heavenly Father has such a radical and overwhelming love for each of us that He sent His one and only Son on a rescue mission – one that would require his Son to shed His blood and to willingly lay down His life for us. Jesus is the only person who is sinless and without blame. Because He is holy and pure, He was able to pay the price for our sins and to exchange His life for our freedom and redemption. That is a truly sacrificial love!

Each person must come before the Lord individually with a sincere, humble, and repentant heart that recognizes their sin and the need for our Savior, Jesus. If we could "earn" our way into heaven or be a "good enough" person, we would have no need for a savior. The death of Jesus on the cross at Calvary would have been unnecessary. But God is very clear that our "good works" cannot atone for our sins and provide a way into heaven and the presence of a Holy God. The scriptures clearly tell us that there is only one way to be "saved" from our sins - it is by grace that a person is saved through faith and not by their own doing; it is the gift of God, not a result of works (from Ephesians 2:8-9). Whoever believes in the Son (Jesus) has eternal life, but whoever rejects the Son will not see life, for God's wrath remains on them (from John 3:36 NIV). In the Gospel of John, Jesus said, "Very truly, I tell you, no one can see the Kingdom of God unless they are born again" (from John 3:3 NIV).

Please join me in praying this most important prayer for our children.

Praying for the Salvation of Your Children

Heavenly Father,

I pray that the hearts of my children would be softened and that they would be able to be sensitive to the Holy Spirit and be convicted of their sins. Let them feel the heaviness and darkness that unforgiven sin brings into their lives. Let them despair over their brokenness and long to be in Your loving presence and to receive Your forgiveness. Because of Your mercy and goodness, Lord, give them a new heart and a new spirit (from Ezekiel 36:26 ESV). May they come to You with sincere, humble, and repentant hearts that confess their sins and their need for a savior. Let them call on the name of the Lord for their salvation (from Romans 10:13 ESV). Let them profess their faith with their mouths and believe in their heart that your Son, Jesus, is Savior and Lord (from Romans 10:10 NIV). May they surrender their lives to You and love You with all their heart, mind, soul, and strength. As they grow in their faith, Your grace that offers salvation will teach them to say no to ungodliness and worldly passions, and to live self-controlled, upright and godly lives (from Titus 2:11-12 NIV). My children will abound in good works because their lives are consecrated and set apart for You. Good deeds and dedicated service to others will be evident in their lives as a result of their faith in You. But may they never be deceived by the enemy that they have earned their salvation, for it is by grace they have been saved through faith and not by their works (from Ephesians 2:8-9 NIV). Even though my children have yet to see You with their eyes, may they love You and believe in You wholeheartedly. Let them be filled with an inexpressible and glorious joy for receiving the end result of their faith, the salvation of their souls (from 1 Peter 1:8-9 NIV).

In the precious and holy name of Jesus, I pray. Amen.

Scriptures About Salvation

For God so loved the world that He gave His one and only Son, that whoever believes in Him shall not perish but have eternal life. (John 3:16 NIV)

For by grace you have been saved through faith, and this is not your own doing; it is the gift of God, not a result of works, so that no one may boast. (Ephesians 2:8-9 ESV)

For all have sinned and fall short of the glory of God. (Romans 3:23 NIV)

I do not set aside the grace of God, for if righteousness could be gained through the law, Christ died for nothing. (Galatians 2:21 NIV)

Everyone who calls on the name of the Lord will be saved. (Romans 10:13 ESV)

Salvation is found in no one else, for there is no other name under heaven given to mankind by which we might be saved. (Acts 4:12 NIV)

He saved us, not because of righteous things we had done, but because of His mercy. He saved us through the washing of rebirth and renewal by the Holy Spirit. (Titus 3:5 NIV)

I am the gate; whoever enters through Me will be saved. (John 10:9 NIV)

Whoever has the Son has life; whoever does not have the Son of God does not have life. (1 John 5:12 ESV)

As far as the east is from the west, so far He has removed our transgressions (sins) from us. (Psalm 103:12 ESV)

For it is with your heart that you believe and are justified, and it is with your mouth that you profess your faith and are saved. (Romans 10:10 NIV)

The Lord is not slow in keeping His promise, as some understand slowness. Instead, He is patient with you, not wanting anyone to perish, but everyone to come to repentance. (2 Peter 3:9 NIV)

So, Christ was sacrificed once to take away the sins of many; and He will appear a second time, not to bear sin, but to bring salvation to those who are waiting for Him. (Hebrews 9:28 NIV)

For the message of the cross is foolishness to those who are perishing, but to us who are being saved, it is the power of God. (1 Corinthians 1:18 NIV)

Whoever believes in the Son has eternal life, but whoever rejects the Son will not see life, for God's wrath remains in them. (John 3:36 NIV)

Truly He is my rock and my salvation; He is my fortress; I will never be shaken. (Psalm 62:2 NIV)

THIS IS NOT GOODBYE!

Just because you came to the end of this prayer challenge does not mean that this is goodbye! May you continue to join me and other moms, day after day, week after week, month after month in covering your kids in prayer. This is not a one-time deal! Nope. My hope is that when you finish these 21 days of prayer and praise, you are committed to being a praying & praising mama for as long as you have breath in you!

You can join me and other moms in the Facebook Group: **Praying & Praising Mamas** for even more encouragement, fellowship, and fun! Be sure to email me at carol.lee.writes@gmail.com if you are interested in having me speak at your women's retreat or conference. Finally, if this book has been an encouragement to you, could you please kindly leave a review on Amazon for Praying & Praising Mama? Many hearty thanks to you!

May you continue to pray big, bold prayers and praise with your whole heart! God is in our midst and He is mighty to save!

Let's Connect!

Website: www.carolleerichardson.com
Instagram: carol.lee.richardson
Facebook Group: Praying & Praising Mamas
Email: carol.lee.writes@gmail.com

More Inspirational Insights

"The wonderful thing about praying is that you leave a world of not being able to do something and enter God's realm where everything is possible. He specializes in the impossible. Nothing is too great for His almighty power. Nothing is too small for His love."

~ Corrie Ten Boom

"If you want that splendid power in prayer, you must remain in loving, living, lasting, conscious, practical, abiding union with the Lord Jesus Christ."

~ Charles Spurgeon

"Our God has boundless resources. The only limit is in us. Our asking, our thinking, our praying are too small. Our expectations are too limited."

~ A.B. Simpson

"Walking with God down the avenue of prayer, we acquire something of His likeness and unconsciously we become witnesses to others of His beauty and His grace."

~ Edward McKendree Bounds

"The greatest tragedy of life is not unanswered prayer, but unoffered prayer."

~ F.B. Meyer

"Is prayer your steering wheel or your spare tire?

~ Corrie Ten Boom

"God shapes the world by prayer. Prayers are deathless. The lips that uttered them may be closed to death, the heart that felt them may have ceased to beat, but the prayers live before God, and God's heart is set on them and the prayers outlive the lives of those who uttered them; they outlive a generation, outlive an age, outlive a world."

~ Edward McKendree Bounds

"Prayer is a strong wall and fortress of the church; it is a goodly Christian weapon."

~ Martin Luther

"Never be afraid to trust an unknown future to a known God."

~ Corrie Ten Boom

"Thanksgiving is inseparable from true prayers; it is almost essentially connected with it. One who always prays is ever giving praise, whether in ease or in pain, both for prosperity and for the greatest adversity. He blesses God for all things."

~ John Wesley

"Four things let us keep in mind: God hears prayers, God heeds prayer, God answers prayer, and God delivers by prayer."

~ Edward McKendree Bounds

"Prayer and praise are the oars by which a man may row his boat into the deep waters of the knowledge of Christ."

~ Charles Spurgeon

"Satan laughs at our toil, mocks at our wisdom, but trembles when we pray."

~ Samuel Chadwick

"What wings are to a bird, and sails to a ship, so is prayer to the soul."

~ Corrie Ten Boom

"Each time before you intercede, be quiet first, and worship God in His glory. Think of what He can do, and how He delights to hear the prayers of His redeemed people. Think of your place and privilege in Christ and expect great things!"

~ Andrew Murray

"Perhaps it takes purer faith to praise God for unrealized blessings than for those we once enjoyed or those we enjoy now."

~ A.W. Tozer

"Answered prayer is the interchange of love between the Father and His child."

~ Andrew Murray

"Only when holiness and worship meet can evil be conquered."

~ Ravi Zacharias

"Prayer is the most sacred occupation a person could engage in."

~ A.W. Tozer

"Trust perfected is prayer perfected. Trust looks to receive the thing asked for and gets it. Trust is not a belief that God can bless or that He will bless, but that He does bless, here and now. Trust always operates in the present tense. Hope looks toward the future. Trust looks to the present. Hope expects. Trust possesses. Trust receives what prayer acquires. So, what prayer needs, at all times, is abiding and abundant trust."

~ Edward McKendree Bounds

"When a Christian shuns fellowship with other Christians, the devil smiles. When he stops studying the Bible, the devil laughs. When he stops praying, the devil shouts for joy.

~ Corrie Ten Boom

"We must begin to believe that God, in the mystery of prayer has entrusted us with a force that can move the Heavenly world and can bring its power down to earth."

~ Andrew Murray

"The Christian's heart must be soaked in prayer before the true spiritual fruits begin to grow."

~ A.W. Tozer

"Grant that I may not pray alone with the mouth; help me that I may pray from the depths of my heart."

~ Martin Luther

"Negligence in prayer withers the inner man. Nothing can be a substitute for it, not even Christian work. Many are so preoccupied with work that they allow little time for prayer. Hence, they cannot cast out demons. Prayer enables us first inwardly to overcome the enemy and then outwardly to deal with him."

~ Watchman Nee

"It takes us long to learn that prayer is more important than organization, more powerful than armies, more influential than wealth and mightier than all learning."

~ Samuel Chadwick

"Mind how you pray. Make real business of it. Let it never be a dead formality... plead the promise in a truthful, business-like way... Ask for what you want, because the Lord has promised it. Believe that you have the blessing and go forth to your work in full assurance of it. Go from your knees singing, because the promise is fulfilled; thus will your prayer be answered... the strength (not length) of your prayers... wins God; and the strength of prayer lies in your faith in the promise which you pleaded before the Lord."

~ Charles Spurgeon

BIBLIOGRAPHY

Abraham Lincoln. (n.d.). AZQuotes.com Retrieved April 10, 2020, from AZQuotes.com Web site: https://www.azquotes.com/quote/176092

A.B. Simpson. (n.d.). AZQuotes.com Retrieved April 10, 2020, from AZQuotes.com Web site: https://www.azquotes.com/author/20446-A_B_Simpson

Aiden Wilson Tozer. (n.d.). AZQuotes.com Retrieved April 10, 2020, from AZQuotes.com Web site: https://www.azquotes.com/author/14750-Aiden_Wilson_Tozer

Andrew Murray. (n.d.). AZQuotes.com Retrieved April 10, 2020, from AZQuotes.com Web site: https://www.azquotes.com/author/18770-Andrew_Murray

Charles Spurgeon. (n.d.). AZQuotes.com Retrieved April 10, 2020, from AZQuotes.com Web site: https://www.azquotes.com/author/13978-Charles_Spurgeon

Corrie Ten Boom. (n.d.). AZQuotes.com Retrieved April 10, 2020, from AZQuotes.com Web site: https://www.azquotes.com/author/1659-Corrie_Ten_Boom

Edward McKendree Bounds. (n.d.). AZQuotes.com Retrieved April 10, 2020, from AZQuotes.com Web site: https://www.azquotes.com/author/21403-Edward_McKendree_Bounds

F.B. Meyer. (n.d.). AZQuotes.com Retrieved April 10, 2020, from AZQuotes.com Web site: https://www.azquotes.com/author/19129-F_B_Meyer

John Bunyan. (n.d.). AZQuotes.com Retrieved April 10, 2020, from AZQuotes.com Web site: https://www.azquotes.com/quotes/491595

John Wesley. (n.d.). AZQuotes.com Retrieved April 10, 2020, from AZQuotes.com Web site: https://www.azquotes.com/author/15507-John_Wesley

Martin Luther. (n.d.). AZQuotes.com Retrieved April 10, 2020, from AZQuotes.com Web site: https://www.azquotes.com/author/9142-Martin_Luther

Ravi Zacharias. (n.d.). AZQuotes.com Retrieved April 10, 2020, from AZQuotes.com Web site: https://www.azquotes.com/author/16119-Ravi_Zacharias

Samuel Chadwick. (n.d.). AZQuotes.com Retrieved April 10, 2020, from AZQuotes.com Web site: https:// www.azquotes.com/author/24160-Samuel_Chadwick

Watchman Nee. (n.d.). AZQuotes.com Retrieved April 10, 2020, from AZQuotes.com Web site: https://www.azquotes.com/author/18200-Watchman_Lee

ABOUT THE AUTHOR

Carol Lee Richardson is a praying & praising mama of three. She finds joy in helping others and is passionate about encouraging women to lead faith-filled, prayerful lives. She holds a Bachelor's Degree in Communication Arts and went on to earn a Master's Degree in Counseling. Carol served previously as a communications officer in the Army National Guard and as a writer & editorial assistant for the National Guard Magazine. After her time in the Army, her main mission was being a stay-at-home mom and homeschooling her children. More recently, she has worked with foster children as a family support counselor and case manager at a faith-based organization. Carol serves as the prayer coordinator at her church and has the privilege of praying with a dedicated group of women affectionately known as the "special forces" prayer warriors.

Made in the USA
Middletown, DE
13 September 2023

38436627R00066